GREAT RUBBER STAMPING

GREAT
RUBBER
STAMPING

Ideas, Tips & Techniques

JUDY RITCHIE AND JAMIE KILMARTIN

HUGH LAUTER LEVIN ASSOCIATES, INC.

Project Director: Leslie Conron Carola
Design: Kathleen Herlihy-Paoli
Writers: John Kelsey and Laura Tringali
Copy Editor: Deborah Zindell
Rubber stamp projects created by Judy Ritchie and / or
Jame Kilmartin unless otherwise
noted in the captions.

CONTENTS

INTRODUCTION

The key to successful rubber stamping is simple: Enjoy what you're doing. As you'll see in the following pages, imperfections in technique are sometimes at the heart of the prettiest designs, and there's really not a whole lot that can go wrong with this versatile art. Don't pressure yourself to produce or to create perfection—if you feel stressed, you're doing something wrong! Remember, along with being creative, stamping can be a fun and relaxing activity, a great antidote to the hustle and bustle of everyday life.

What could be simpler than this lovely flower stamped on plain paper, layered onto a slightly larger piece of contrasting background? The collage seems more complex, but each element is just a stamp, a charm, or a dried flower arranged in a way.

W̲e have arranged the projects in *Great Rubber Stamping: Ideas, Tips & Techniques* into categories—simple stamping, paper, color, backgrounds and frames, embossing, punch art, and special effects (including embellishments, 3-D artwork, and a collection of unique surfaces and challenges). As you'll soon see, many of the projects were created using a number of techniques, and therefore could be equally at home in a number of different categories. We've tried to coordinate the best examples of different aspects of a technique in each category. As you leaf through the projects, you'll find much that is familiar even as you're exploring new ideas and techniques. For each project featured you'll find instructions on the way we made the project, which you can follow to the letter, or use as a springboard to get the idea for a creation that is uniquely your own. We are merely offering ideas and techniques—you can interweave them however you wish!

Along with the well over one hundred featured projects for which we have included instructions there are also many variations on a theme—projects that offer a similar technique or effect, or simply offer further visual information for you to consider. We want to flood your vision with lots of ideas and keep you observing and thinking creatively. Remember, you can make a project as simple or complicated as you like.

Once everything is organized, you've read the introductory sections of this book, and you have your basic materials on hand, how do you actually begin to rubber stamp? Simple—jump right in and make somebody a card. In this day of the mass-produced, the handmade becomes increasingly special, and a hand-crafted card or paper gift will no doubt brighten the day of anybody you care about. As you get into the swing of things, you might want to make some time to create a supply of greeting cards, so you'll have some to send during the busy times of your life.

Birthday cards, thank-you cards, holiday cards, even gift bags and tags can all be made well in advance and stored for when you need them. But, of course, there is nothing like creating a card or gift *just* for someone special *just* for a special occasion. When you have the essential tools on hand and you feel comfortable working with them there is nothing to stop spontaneous creative output. Being prepared is a good thing! The beauty of rubber stamping is that once you get started, it's nearly impossible to stop, and you'll soon find opportunities for stamping everything from bulletin-board notices to recipe cards.

Once you get started, you can make a variety of projects using rubber stamps with contemporary stamping materials. The gingerbread man features "icing" made with white gel pen; the birds triptych gets its professional polish from black embossing ink.

BASIC STAMPING

*T*he supplies you will need for basic stamping are few: stamps, ink, and paper. If you're a novice, there's a good way to start up: Begin by selecting some white and cream paper, then choose two or three colors of paper that will work together. Select a few inks to complement the colored papers. By following this simple plan, you'll create a functional palette that will allow enormous design flexibility.

*I*f you add some extras to your toolbox—some decorative cutting tools and embossing supplies, for example— you'll be ready to follow your imagination wherever it takes wing. As experienced stampers know, the sky's the limit when you stroll the aisles of your favorite craft or stamp-supply store, but also expect your interest to pique when you look with a stamper's eye at things you already have around your home. You'll be surprised how ordinary everyday objects can find an artful place in your projects.

The art of rubber stamping has evolved to the point where vast quantities of stamping products fill the aisles of craft and stamp-supply stores. To make things more confusing,

every time you enter a store, there seems to be an array of newer and better products promising the moon. In a well-stocked store you'll find it all, from tassel-making tools and scented embossing powders to hand-held bulb syringes that let you replicate air-brushed effects with markers. Are all these products fun? Yes. Are they all useful? Probably. Are they all necessary? Certainly not. As you'll see again and again in this book, stunning effects can be created with the simplest of products. There's no need for you to feel that you must buy all that your supplier offers, especially when you are just getting started. As you add skills and your creativity blossoms, you can buy what you need as you need it.

STAMPS

*S*tamp images number in the thousands, and while you will be tempted to collect them all, keep in mind that you can really stretch your stamping budget by thinking up ways to get multiple images from a simple stamp. Learn to see beyond the whole shape to its individual elements.

The workhorses of your stamp collection will most likely be wood-mounted stamps, consisting of a rubber die mounted to a foam cushion, which in turn is glued to the

wood block. You'll probably also use foam-backed rubber stamps. These are typically sold in sets of related images or themes (such as alphabet letters or animals), and are less expensive than wood-mounted stamps. They're versatile, but lacking the rigid platform of a wood-mounted stamp, it can be hard to gauge the right pressure for a clear impression. Rubber stamps also come mounted on see-through plastic, which can simplify the task of positioning a stamp in a design. You can always mount stamps on

Seeing beyond a whole stamp to its individual parts will help you use your stamps to fullest advantage. Here, the whole stamp is central, while the rosebud part is used for the background.

A carved rubber stamp may not always be the perfect answer to a design question, so undoubtedly you'll eventually want to experiment with roller stamps and stylus tools. A roller stamp prints a line of images as you roll it across the surface. It's great for frames, backgrounds, and borders, and is as easy to use as a paint roller. Stylus tools have interchangeable shaped tips that are made from a soft white or a dense black foam. They are ideal for stamping, stenciling, brushing, and color patterning. The white foam tip is designed for blending inks on paper or stenciling. Since the black foam is denser, it is more effectively used as a stamp because it leaves a more distinct image. Also, you can also mold the black foam tip to different shapes. Just heat the tip with a light bulb (actually touch the tip to the bulb) for twenty seconds, then press down for ten seconds on any textured surface—for example, leaves, lace, or a portion of a rubber stamp. The stylus will pick up the image, which you can then stamp. To remove the impression and remold a new one, simply reheat the stylus tip. Tempted to use a heat gun for this? Don't. The heat may melt any plastic parts of the stylus.

blocks of wood. You might consider mounting a wooden block yourself. This is very easy to do. First, you need a cushion between the rubber die and the mount. There are cushions designed specifically for rubber-stamp mounting, but you can also use craft foam, or even foam shoe inserts. For mounts, consider scraps of wood, wooden blocks, plastic boxes, empty thread spools, or empty jars. To begin, firmly pull the rubber die from the foam mounting and trim the die using scissors. Cut close to the design, but be careful not to undercut the image. Use rubber cement to mount the stamp to the cushion. Once the glue has set, cut the cushion to the same size or a bit larger than the die. Then, again using rubber cement, attach the cushion and stamp to your mount. Be sure that the die is parallel to the straight edge of the mount.

The honeycomb background of this card was made with a hexagon-shaped stylus tool and several inks.

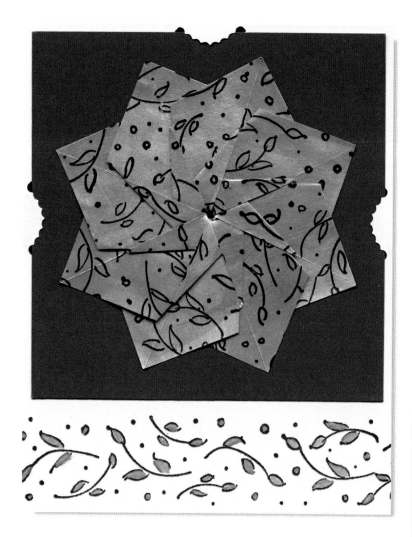

Besides stamps, ink, and paper, you can use many different art supplies and household materials in stamping projects. At left, the star consists of eight plain paper squares painted blue and stamped with flowers using a rollograph. Below, a sprig of dried flowers has been layered onto two squares made with block stamps.

Stamping with sponges (both man-made and natural sea sponges) is another way to create some interesting impressions. Depending on texture, sponges can print everything from dense sweeps of color to wispy clouds. And while not strictly a stamp, a brayer is invaluable for spreading color rapidly across a surface. Brayers come with either hard rubber or sponge rollers: both types can be inked with patterns ranging from herringbones to plaids and transferred to paper.

On the home front, you'll probably find plenty of objects that make interesting stamped images. Try a carved potato or other root vegetable, a halved grapefruit, a crumpled newsprint scrap, a leaf, a flower, or a coiled piece of string glued to cardboard. If you like, you can carve your own rubber stamp from a large eraser or piece of cork. Don't be afraid to stretch your imagination. If something looks like it might make a good stamp, try it.

INKS AND COLORING TOOLS

You can use your stamps with many colorants (and of course you can add all kinds of color to a card after you stamp the image). For clear impressions and easy cleanup, nothing beats pigment and dye inks. Pigment ink, which is made from ground particles of color, is thick like paint. It's slow to dry because it sits on top of the paper rather than being absorbed. The slow-drying quality of pigment ink makes it invaluable for blending colors and embossing; its opacity means you can use pigment inks on any color of paper without affecting the color of the ink. (If you want to stamp with pigment ink on glossy or coated papers, which are nonabsorbent, you must emboss the ink to make it permanent.) Pigment ink is also light-fast, which may be an important quality when you know an artwork will be exposed to sunlight. Pads of pigment ink are available in a vast selection of colors plus metallics. Small, shaped ink pads (called cat's eyes), and lipstick-tube-type containers (called daubers), are use-ful when you want to apply colors selectively to a stamp. When the ink on the pad runs dry, all pads may be refreshed with re-inkers, or bottled ink.

Dye ink contains no particles of color, so it's thinner than pigment ink. Dye ink dries more rapidly, and whereas pigment ink is opaque when it dries, dye ink dries translucent. While the quick-drying time may get in the way of blending or embossing colors, you can use the properties of dye ink to your advantage to add dimension to an artwork by building up layers of color. Another advantage of dye ink is that it works on almost any type of paper. Like pigment ink, dye ink comes in markers and in small and large ink pads. Re-inkers are available to replenish pads.

Archival inks, developed originally for the scrapbook enthusiast, have become popular with stampers, although they are not available in as many colors as water-based

Sometimes you'll want to paint the stamped image with watercolors, while other times you'll color the paper before punching, as with the leaves at right.

dye and pigment inks. Archival inks become permanent once stamped on either porous or coated paper. Therefore, they are perfect to use when you want to color with water-based markers or watercolors after you have stamped. Although the ink will come off your stamp with water if cleaned immediately, it is more difficult to remove than dye or pigment inks and may stain the rubber.

A solvent-based ink is one that will dry on any surface, such as clear window plastic or shrink plastic, but requires a stamp cleaner specifically designed for this ink. There are other inks, referred to as crafters inks, that will dry on these nonporous surfaces as well as paper, but they require heat-setting.

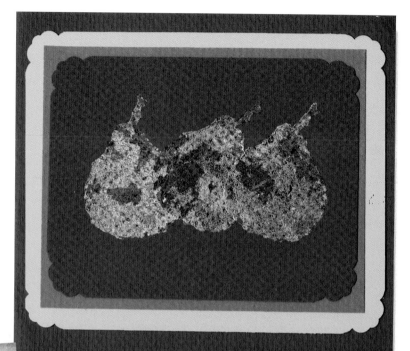

Color doesn't have to come from ink. Here, the colored cardstock flickers through the gold-leafed image of three pears. Metallic leaf is so thin that it usually interacts with the background color.

Dye-based inks are translucent, so they can be combined on the paper like watercolors, as shown left. Pigment inks, which dry more slowly than dye inks, are opaque because they contain particles of paint.

The words and the embossed snowflakes on the mittens are the only stamped element on this pretty card. The mittens themselves are punched out of colored paper, the cuffs are liquid appliqué, the tie is twisted rope with a small metallic brad.

Colored pencils, chalks, and watercolor paint and markers all add charm and character to stamped artworks. Besides using them to produce lovely detailed designs, use them to douse with color the broad, empty spaces of "open" stamps, those images that are mainly outline, like pictures in a coloring book. Colored pencils can be used to give a project a soft, muted appearance or to build up gradations of color. Since outlines of the pencil strokes usually remain, you'll add texture as well as color to the paper. Unlike colored pencils, chalks blend together into a soft, continuous finish that is suggestive of watercolors without watercolor's trademark transparency. Because chalk leaves behind a delicate finish, preserve its color with a workable fixative. Watercolors are fun to blend right out of the paintbox, but the color from watercolor markers can be fairly aggressive—if you like, tone it down a bit by applying the color to the stamp with a brush rather than the marker tip.

You can also stamp with various acrylic paints and inks by applying them to the stamp with foam brushes or sponges, or by creating a pad with a piece of flat foam. Because of the nature of acrylic paint, wash the foam or brushes before the paint dries.

Some specialized materials can give your project a kick of color, texture, or shine. Dry powder pigments can be used to add color to watermark inks or ultra-thick and special-effects embossing powders; you can also add them to gum arabic to create paint. Iridescent, pearlized, and glitter paints and inks are available to paint in a stamped image or to color paper. They can also be used for interesting sponged backgrounds. Liquid appliqué can add color and texture to a project, since it puffs up when heated. Dimensional adhesives can be purchased clear to create a shiny raised finish when dry, or you can add glitter

..LET IT SNOW...LET IT SNOW...LET IT SNOW!

or color. Pre-colored dimensional adhesives come in small squeeze bottles with fine nib dispenser tips. Some come with glitter and others dry to an opalescent finish. They can be used to write or embellish images.

Gold leafing comes in full 5 1/2-inch leaves as well as in flakes. Both the leaves and flakes are available in various colors. Leafing can be applied to glue that has become tacky or to sheets of adhesive. You can stamp using glue as an ink and, once it's tacky, apply the leafing flakes to it. Or you can brush the adhesive on an image or article and apply the leafing. Once the leafing covers the adhesive, brush the excess off with a firm, flat stenciling brush. Save the excess flakes for future application.

EMBOSSING

At the heart of the embossing process is embossing powder, the stuff you sprinkle into the wet ink and heat with a heat gun until it rises from the surface. Embossing powders come in clear—which lets the color of your ink shine through—as well as in a variety of colors, textures, metallics, and pearlescents. Detail embossing powder is formulated to stick to fine inked lines (although it doesn't rise as high as regular powder), while extra-thick embossing powder is made to be layered into heavy lines.

Embossing powder works best with pigment ink, because its slow drying time allows you plenty of time to work. You can also use special embossing ink, a thick, glycerin-based substance that comes tinted as well as clear and opaque. Embossing pens are good for detail work, but they dry quickly so you'll have to work fast. Don't have an embossing pen? Substitute a fine-line erasable ink pen. It really does work.

Embossing powder rises from the surface under heat, so you'll need a heat source. A toaster oven set to 300 degrees or an iron set to "cotton" will do the job, but you'll never get enough heat from a hair dryer. If you plan to do a lot of embossing, invest in a small heat gun sold for the purpose. You'll appreciate its safety and convenience.

Since the process of embossing requires you to shake excess powder off the inked design, plan to somehow capture the loose powder and get it back into the jar. Take steps to conserve your embossing powder and a jar will last a long time.

Embossed images rise from the paper and shine. The basic technique is to stamp the image, sprinkle with embossing powder, and heat.

MASKING AND
POP-UP TECHNIQUES

A versatile but simple technique for creating special effects is masking. Masking allows you to control where the ink goes on a project—onto the surface in unmasked areas, off the surface anywhere that's masked. Masking can be used in all sorts of situations, from stamping a series of background images right up to the border of the central image to stamping images one in front of another to create a scene with a distinct foreground and background. In all cases, masking gives an artwork the illusion of depth.

There are two popular forms of masks. The first mask blocks out the stamped main image. The second, a mortise mask, blocks out all *but* the main image. A mortise mask uses the negative space left by cutting out of your masking material the shape of the image to be masked. It is, in fact, a template.

Masks help control where the ink hits the paper, and where it does not. At left, the mask blocked out the flower stamp; above, a mortise mask kept the dots and flowers on the wrapping paper.

Masks can be made from paper by stamping the image on a piece of scrap and cutting out the image to its outline. (For ease in handling, you could leave a paper "tail" on the mask by which to hold the mask in place over the stamped image.)

The mask is positioned over the area to be protected from receiving more ink. The mask should be cut slightly smaller than the area you want to keep free of ink. The thickness of the masking paper prevents the ink from stamping near the edge of the mask.

You can also mask areas of the project surface by stamping one or more images with a clear resist pad or by stamping with clear embossing ink and embossing with a clear powder. When you color the surface with a brayer or other tools, the images will be revealed in stark contrast to the colored background.

Pop-up cards are simple to execute and are guaranteed to surprise and please. Select a stamp that will fit within the dimensions of the card you are designing. The easiest pop-up base to construct is a platform cut from the card itself. With a card closed, determine where you want your selected image placed. Cut two parallel slits across the fold and pull the cut-out portion forward and then fold it back and crease. Now open the card and press the middle cut piece up from behind to create the platform.

Pop-up cards are always a delight. At left, dogs of all kinds send their belated but sincere wishes, and above, children from many nations pop up from a globe-shaped card with their greeting.

ADHESIVES

Many of your projects will require some sort of glue to hold parts together. A high-performance crafters glue is a must for gluing heavier papers and adding embellishments, but you'll also want glue sticks and pens on hand for layering lighter papers and adding glitters. Like paper, glue can be archival, designed for use with projects that you make as keepsakes. Foam mounting tape and dots are great for lifting a stamped image above the background and giving dimension to a project. These double-sided adhesives can turn even a simple project into something special. Regular cellophane tape also has a place in a stamper's arsenal of adhesives. The glue you use depends on the project, and you should experiment until you find what works best for you.

Glue and other adhesive materials hold most stamped projects together. At right, the punched-out flower parts have been glued together atop the card. Below, a stamped border was glued onto lush textured cardstock.

TOOLS FOR ACCURACY AND CUTTING

*T*here are a variety of tools that will allow you to execute your ideas on paper and other surfaces with great accuracy. You'll really appreciate a stamp positioner when you're trying to combine stamps, such as adding leaves to a stamped flower stem. Additionally, a stamp positioner will help you stamp a straight border, salvage an unclear image by allowing you to precisely re-stamp over it, or deepen a stamped image by over-stamping in a different color.

A stamp positioner is simply a L- or T-shaped piece of clear plastic that provides a firm edge for placing your stamps. You use it with tracing paper or a flat piece of clear plastic. You fit the paper into the corner, being careful not to slide it under the positioner, then slide the stamp along one of the sides of the positioner—when the stamp fits snugly into the corner, stamp on the paper. Remove the positioner, and place the stamped tracing paper over your cardstock to see where you want the image placed. Once identified, bring the positioner back into place next to the tracing paper. Remove the paper and, using the positioner as a guide, stamp the image.

Templates are stencils—cutouts in paper or plastic that confine your stampings to the template shape, resulting in a crisp, clean image. Templates are particularly useful with small stamps, because you can create a big, bold image just by re-stamping in the "live", or open, area of the stencil. You can buy templates in a variety of shapes or make your own by cutting mat board with a sharp X-Acto knife. Cut along a metal ruler for straight lines, freehand (or along shaped objects like cans or bottles, for example) for curves.

If you're making greeting cards, you'll soon find that a bone folder is a useful tool. This simple tool scores a crisp, accurate crease in the paper for easy folding.

A sharp pair of straight scissors is a must, but you'll probably want to own a few of the many decorative-edged scissors that are on the market. Scallop- and deckle-edge scissors are two popular types. Rotary cutters, which look like small pizza cutters, are also useful for cutting decorative edges. In addition to these tools, most stampers keep an X-Acto knife and a supply of blades on hand. A

You will most likely rely on a pair of deckle-edge scissors time and time again to add visual interest to a stamped project. The gently-textured edge contributes to the refined finishing on this simple effective card.

self-healing cutting mat provides a smooth and safe surface for cutting, and won't scar so you can use it for a long time. It also makes a great surface for stamping.

Punches are hand-held devices used to cut shapes from paper. Corner punches, hole punches, and shaped punches all can be used to add charm and character to stamped artworks.

A corrugator, sometimes called a crimper, doesn't cut the paper like scissors or a paper punch, but it does shape it. Because the ridges are on both sides of the paper, handmade corrugated paper must be carefully handled so the ridges don't flatten.

Punches and decorative paper edgers allow you to scallop edges, punch shapes, and generally enhance confections like this gingerbread house.

STAMPING TECHNIQUE

Clarity of image is a primary goal of every stamp artist. There are certain techniques that seem like second-nature to experienced stampers, but novices may need a little practice to get a polished look.

Stamping is a two-handed job. One hand holds the stamp in position on the paper while the other applies pressure. The amount of pressure you apply really depends on the stamp. As a rule of thumb, the larger the stamp, and the more solid the stamping image on the rubber, the harder you will have to press. Since each stamp is cut differently, it never hurts, when working with a new stamp, to do a few test runs on scrap paper. You may find that one part of a stamp needs more or less pressure than another part. This knowledge can help you conserve your good paper.

To transfer the image to the paper, run the fingertips of your "pressure" hand firmly and evenly over the entire surface of the stamp. Avoid rocking the stamp or the image might come out fuzzy. If you're stamping a greeting card, open it first and lay it flat so the ink will adhere as evenly close to the fold as it does elsewhere; you might want to mask off the back to get a crisp, clean edge. If stamping an envelope, your image will be crisper if you insert a slip of cardboard under the area of the envelope to be stamped. Always open your cards and lay them flat

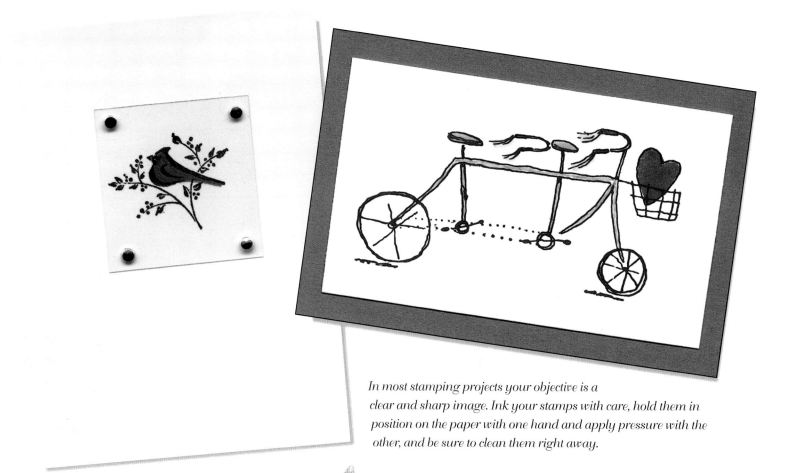

In most stamping projects your objective is a clear and sharp image. Ink your stamps with care, hold them in position on the paper with one hand and apply pressure with the other, and be sure to clean them right away.

so you have an even surface on which to stamp. If you try to stamp with the card folded, the ink may not adhere properly at the double-folded edge of the card.

The surface on which you stamp is as important to a good impression as your tools, materials, and technique. It should be flat, even, and somewhat cushiony. Good surfaces are a self-healing cutting mat, an old mouse pad, a pad of newsprint, or an old magazine.

Don't expect great results from your stamping efforts every single time. Inevitably you will encounter smudges, blurs, incomplete inking, and who knows what else. The trick is to view these incidents as opportunities for advancing your technique—and your creativity. For example, smudges will disappear if you incorporate them into a sponged background. Blurry images can be covered up in all sorts of ways, from attaching a new stamped image directly over the stamped image to elevating a new image above the old on adhesive foam strips or dots. Embellishments such as charms or ribbons are another great way to cover up mistakes, and incomplete inkings can often be rescued with fine-tip markers. Look carefully at what you've produced before you decide what to do with it.

INKING A STAMP WITH A PAD

Before you can practice your stamping technique, you need to load your stamp with ink. There are two ways to apply ink from a pad. The first way is to hold the stamp, image up, in one hand and the inkpad in the other. Lightly tap the inkpad on the stamp several times. The second way is to lightly tap the stamp onto the inkpad several times. With either method, turn the stamp in the light occasionally as you work, to reveal uninked areas. Gently ink those spots, making sure not to over-ink the rest of the stamp.

Most rubber stampers prefer to tap the inkpad onto the stamp instead of the other way around when using a large stamp. You might find it more difficult to judge pressure when you tap the stamp onto the pad, and there always seems to be the tendency to press a little too hard. This excess pressure will cause the ink to well up and fill in the stamp, which may cause blurriness and a loss of

The leaf stamp at the center was inked with several cat's-eye pads; the same stamp was then used to stamp the background. The color under the leafy images was made by a stylus directly on the paper.

save this inking method for small stamps or touchups.

Small stamp pads, cat's eyes, and dauber tools let you control the application of ink and also allow for selective inking, the technique of coloring only one area of a stamp and using it in combination with other stamps. Selective inking is a terrific way to maximize the use of the stamps in a small collection. Suppose, for example, that you have a stamp that pictures a greeting, a watering can, and a bouquet of flowers. Through selective inking, you can use some or all of these elements separately to create a variety of different projects.

detail when the stamp is pressed to paper. Over-inking by a bit isn't really a big deal—just gently press off the extra ink on scrap before working on the project paper. But if the excess ink is substantial, it's best to clean off your stamp and start fresh. For this reason we generally

INKING A STAMP WITH MARKERS

Markers offer a stamper great flexibility. Of course you can use a single marker to ink an entire stamp, but you can also use several different markers to create a multi-colored impression. Markers also allow selective inking, and are especially good for details that are too small for even small inkpads to handle.

Inking stamps with markers gives you precise control over where the colors go. With the stamp in one hand and a marker in the other, add the color with the side of the marker to cover a large area; use the tip for finer detail. If you're using a number of colors on a single stamp, work from lightest to darkest, so you won't accidentally conta-

minate light colors with dark ones and have to start the whole inking process anew. If your light-colored marker picks up another color, simply sweep the marker across a folded, wet paper towel to remove the color.

While you should look occasionally to make sure you're getting full ink coverage, don't dally while inking or the ink could dry out—as signaled by dull-looking rather than glistening ink. If needed, restore moisture to the ink by breathing on the stamp with an open-mouthed "hah" just before stamping. A light spritz of water from a spray bottle will also restore moisture, but the danger here is that too much water will cause the ink to run.

INKING AND USING A BRAYER

For a solid-color background, inking with a brayer is fast and easy: just roll the brayer over the inkpad several times the same as you would roll a paint roller in a paint tray. When you get to the edge of the inkpad, roll the brayer off with a slight lift. To apply the ink, roll the brayer across the paper in one direction. If streaks appear on the paper, roll over the paper several times, always in the same direction, using overlapping strokes.

You can also use your brayer to create fabulous plaids and patterns. These imprints look like they've taken forever to create, but in fact the technique is a snap. With brush markers, color solid stripes of ink around the roller. Roll the stripes across the paper, then rotate the paper a quarter-turn and re-brayer the paper to create a second set of stripes at right angles to the first. Don't limit yourself to plaids with this technique—many patterns lend themselves to brayering. If you need to, blow on the roller with an open-mouthed "hah" to remoisten the ink. Remember, inking coated paper with a brayer produces the brightest colors.

We used a brayer to pick up color from a rainbow pad to apply to paper before stamping and crimping these autumn leaves.

CLEANUP

A big advantage of using water-based inks is that they're easy to clean off your stamps. Dye inks will usually come right off with a damp paper towel, though pigment inks may need a bit of elbow grease and a small brush along with the water. Never use harsh cleaners on your stamps, because they may dry out the rubber. Stamps that have been used with a solvent-based ink should be cleaned with specially formulated cleaner.

Clean your stamps after each color change. Tap off as much extra ink as possible by stamping on scrap or newsprint. Clean off the rest with a damp paper towel, sponge, or cloth. Dry your stamps with a clean cloth, or by stamping on absorbent paper. Cleaning will be less of a chore if you plan for cleanup as you set up. It's tempting to rush through cleanup, but you'll get the best results the next time when you start with clean stamps.

YOUR WORKSPACE

One of the most important things you can do for yourself as a rubber stamper is to provide yourself with a dedicated workspace. It doesn't have to be very big—a card table in a corner of a bedroom is fine—but it must be yours alone or you'll never get anything done. In addition to being off-limits to children and other adults, your workspace should be neat, free of clutter, and offer sufficient storage for materials, works in progress, and completed projects. If space is tight, you might want to investigate a portable workstation, such as a rolling cabinet with pull-out trays. Lighting is important, too. Artists have traditionally preferred natural north light, but you'll still need some sort of bright task lighting that you can move and adjust.

Sunlight, heat, and dust are the enemies of stamps, because they will dry out the rubber. Proper storage is therefore a must to protect the life of your stamps. At first, when your collection is small, you'll probably be able to fit everything in a shoebox or small plastic container. Translucent plastic boxes are great because you can see the contents from the outside. Eventually you'll need to upgrade to larger bins or boxes, but keep things accessible. Don't fall prey to "toybox syndrome," where everything eventually filters to the bottom of the box in a big jumble. Whatever container you use, make sure the stamps are clean and dry when you put them away. Place stamps in the container flat, with the image side facing down.

Having a small collection of stamps is quite manageable, since you can easily shuffle through your stamps to locate the ones you want (or to spark your imagination if you've forgotten which stamps you own). If you're like most rubber stampers, however, eventually you'll accumulate so many stamps that you'll need to catalog them in some manner. Some people like to sort their stamps by manufacturer, others by image (holiday, frames, flowers, peo-

ple, etc.), or category. Since it can be difficult to keep track of all the stamps you collect, some stampers imprint an image of each stamp they own into a blank book—it's much easier to turn the pages of a book than it is to sort through boxes. If your collection becomes enormous, this will also help keep you from purchasing the same stamp twice, as you can quickly refer to your reference book before buying anything new.

Store stamp pads the same way you store stamps, with their working surfaces down. Store markers flat—horizontal. This will keep the color where you need it. Tightly press down the lids of stamp pads and cap your markers before you put them away. Old mugs make good containers for colored pencils, because you can move them to the work surface as needed, and once positioned, they will keep coloring tools from rolling away. Likewise, store papers flat in a box or tub where they will be protected from dust. Smaller papers fit well in the manila accordion files that are available from office-supply stores.

*Organize you materials well
and you'll be able to find an extra scrap or eyelet to use.*

GREETING CARDS AND ENVELOPES

*T*hough cardstock is offered in conveniently packaged sets of folded cards and matching envelopes, you'll inevitably want to purchase $8^1/2$ x 11 sheets of card stock both for economy and design flexibility. To cut the cardstock to size, use sharp scissors, a mat knife, or, better yet, a paper cutter. Using a straightedge, score a centerline with a stylus or bone folder, then crease the fold. Layer the card as desired.

Envelopes come to fit most card sizes, but you can make your own with envelope templates sold at craft and stamping-supply stores. Making your own envelopes lets you pick the color and type of paper that will best suit a particular card. They're easy to make—you trace the template, score the paper with a blunt-edged tool, cut out the envelope, and fold and burnish the creases. Apply glue to the seams and assemble the envelope. To add a lining, just repeat the above steps with the lining paper, but slightly reduce the size of the lining, so it will fit within the assembled envelope. Don't forget, envelopes aren't just for containing things. A small envelope with a pull-out message can be a charming, interactive decoration for a greeting card.

To line a pre-folded envelope, gently steam the seams open over a pan of hot water and let the paper dry. Trace around the open envelope onto lining paper, then attach the lining paper to the envelope with glue. Refold the envelope and glue the seams. See the chart for some standard envelope and card sizes.

SOME STANDARD ENVELOPE AND CARD SIZES

ENVELOPE Size	SINGLE Card	NARROWFOLD Card	BROADFOLD Card	FRENCH FOLD Sheet (flat)
$4^3/8$ x $5^3/4$	$4^1/4$ x $5^1/2$	$4^1/4$ x 11	$5^1/2$ x $8^1/2$	$8^1/2$ x 11
$4^3/4$ x $6^1/2$	$4^5/8$ x $6^1/4$	$4^1/2$ x $12^1/2$	$6^1/4$ x 9	9 x $12^1/4$
$5^1/4$ x $7^1/4$	$5^1/8$ x 7	5 x 14	7 x 10	10 x 14
$5^1/2$ x $8^1/8$	$5^3/8$ x $7^7/8$	$5^1/4$ x $15^1/2$	$7^3/4$ x $10^1/2$	$10^1/2$ x $15^1/2$
6 x $9^1/2$	$5^7/8$ x $9^1/4$	$5^3/4$ x $18^1/2$	$9^1/4$ x $11^1/2$	$11^1/2$ x $18^1/2$
$3^7/8$ x $8^7/8$	$3^3/4$ x $8^5/8$	$3^3/4$ x $17^1/4$	$7^1/2$ x $8^5/8$	$7^1/2$ x $17^1/4$

Just as you can make a lining for a purchased pre-folded envelope, you can make your own envelopes without a template. Measure the size of your finished, folded card. Make your own template by creating an image just a bit larger overall than your card. Practice a few folds, make some interesting edges. With a few trial and error attempts, you'll be creating beautiful envelopes on your own. Remember to make the envelope just a bit larger than the folded card.

DESIGN

The term design simply means the arrangement of elements on a page—or how you select and organize your materials and images. Good designs don't just happen by themselves. Some-one created them. While there are no firm rules for good design, there are various elements to consider, both by themselves and in combination with other elements. And while it may be difficult to say why one design succeeds and another fails, people usually find it easy to agree on what they like: We know it when we see it. A harmonious design is like harmony in music: it just feels right.

People often think of "design" in terms of basic elements like composition, line, color, and pattern or repetition. But before you get to any of that, it really helps if you set the scene by pausing to deliberately think about the context and the purpose of the project. Feelings matter, too—both yours and the recipient's if the project is to be given to another person.

Ask yourself such questions as, What is the artwork for? Is it a gift, an announcement, a note, a picture for the wall? What is your central message? Is it a hearty "thank you," a heartfelt condolence, or a lighthearted wish for happiness? Who's going to receive it, where will they be, and what else will be going on? And what's the emotional content, that is, how do you feel about your message, and how do you expect or even want the recipient to feel? You'll find it very helpful to jot down your answers, along with any words or images that come to mind while you think. These notes will be a useful checklist you can consult as you develop your design.

While there are no limits, most stamping projects rely on good composition, pleasant rhythms, expressive lines, and harmonious colors. On the following pages we'll take a close look at successful stamping projects that get the most out of these elements.

One stamp, colored pencils, and three colored mats offer a pleasing design.

THE ELEMENTS OF DESIGN

CONTEXT. The one thing that's most important is your personal message and your feelings about it. It's easy to become overwhelmed by the limitless possibilities that rubber stamping offers, and it's easy to become confused by design guidelines. Whenever you have trouble focusing on your message, go back and review your notes to help you align the elements of design with your intentions.

COMPOSITION. What shape is your artwork? How should you arrange your words and images on it? Every composition involves proportion, background and foreground, balance, and focus. There are countless combinations of these basic elements—and every one of them will help to convey a message. Of course, you can't go wrong with a centered composition, especially on a square card. And if you want to create a feeling of direction or motion, try a diagonal composition. Always trust *your* eye to tell you the "right" arrangement of elements for your particular project.

COLOR. The rainbow's your oyster. With today's inks, markers, and stamp pads, there's no limit on your palette. Choosing harmonious colors is the challenge, but you can learn how to do that by working with shades and hues of one color, with complementary colors (colors that are directly opposite each other on the color wheel), and with pairs of colors that are adjacent on the color wheel (called analogous colors).

LINE. Lines of different weight, thickness, and consistency convey different feelings. Where other artists draw the lines they want, stampers usually choose an image that already contains the desired line quality. You can change stamped lines by embossing, by gluing on thread, by over-stamping, or by drawing with marker inks.

RHYTHM AND REPETITION. Repeated visual elements can make a lively background or border as well as create illusions of depth and motion. Stamps make it easy to repeat an image. Remember, a design will usually look better if the repeating images are arranged in an orderly manner, but that doesn't necessarily mean that the images have to move across a page. Left to right, top to bottom, corner to corner, in a circle, or even partially off the page—the same stamp repeated in a different way will give a very different feel to your artwork.

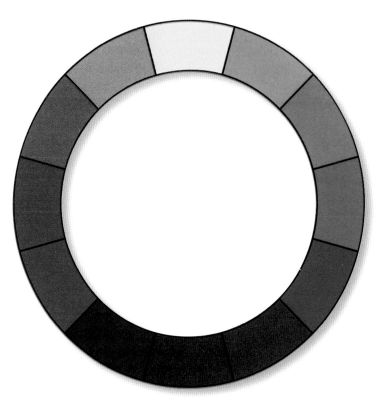

The color wheel is the rainbow arranged in a circle. The primary colors are red, yellow, and blue. Complementary pairs are across from each other, and analogous colors are next to one another.

THINKING ABOUT DESIGN

*L*et's look at several simple card designs to see what makes them work. Use these examples to get some ideas about designs that will work for your artwork.

A RHYTHMIC SQUARE

CONTEXT. This is a blank card, suitable for almost any occasion. The open flowers invite the recipient to open the card, expectantly, to see what's inside.

COMPOSITION. The card itself is a square with the natural focal point at the center. This almost forces the smaller elements to be squares, too.

RHYTHM AND REPETITION. Four same-sized flowers move rhythmically around the square. This technique looks as if it were woven or quilted.

COLOR. The yellow layer works well with the green card—its lightness lifts the design off the card and toward the viewer. The four quilted squares harmonize in soft hues of blue and purple, all adjacent on the color wheel, and make a pleasing background for the black ink.

These cards illustrate the essence of design: stay with similar shapes and harmonious colors, and above all keep it simple. A slight tilt to the snowman's hat and his smile seems wider.

THE JAUNTY SNOWMAN (facing page)

CONTEXT. The jaunty snowman takes his hat off to you to send a friendly greeting, perhaps a thank you, perhaps an invitation to a wintertime event.

COMPOSITION. The blue background card and the white-layered-on-olive central card are both the same rectangular shape, ensuring basic visual harmony. The way the central card swings on its pin is an added bonus, adding motion and visual interest.

RHYTHM AND REPETITION. The artist has stamped the background with large snowflakes spaced roughly the same distance apart. The fact that the spacing is rough gives the card an informal feeling; precise spacing would impart a formal note that might contradict the card's easy message.

LINE. At first glance you might not see any lines in this artwork, but in fact the artist has used line qualities in a number of subtle ways. The snowflakes are drawn with a broad, loose stroke. Even though they don't actually look like real snowflakes (which have six points, whereas these have eight), there is no doubt about what they represent. The snowman is enclosed inside a blue quadrilateral stamped with a partially inked block. This technique makes a crisp outside edge fading to a soft inner one, economically evoking a block of ice, or a window in winter. Finally, the white uninked spirals inside the snowman's body give these simple circles a three-dimensional solidity.

COLOR. With many shades of blue and small orange highlights, this card is an excellent example of a complementary color scheme. Its strength comes from the fact that it's mostly blue, with a very small amount of the complementary orange. It would be interesting to experiment with the color of the central background card. Although the soft olive hue works well, a bright blue, warm green, or burnt orange might be even better.

CHEERY CHERRIES

CONTEXT. Three cherries are a traditional kitchen symbol. They evoke summertime, home, simple pleasures, and a bountiful pantry. The gingham border and stitched line of ribbon reinforce the message, as do the cheery colors.

COMPOSITION. The image is a square, centered in the upper half of a rectangular card. The symmetry is calm and pleasing. The stitched line of ribbon across the bottom of the rectangle is a pleasant addition that fills out the rectangle.

LINE. Sometimes the strongest line is the one that isn't really there. Traditional stencils often use the three-cherries motif, with a wide gap between the stenciled elements. This white space becomes a line that helps give the cherries a three-dimensional quality.

COLOR. Using red for the cherries and for the background card unites this composition. Green is the complement of red, and black, like white, works with everything.

ABUNDANCE IN A SCHOOL OF FISH

COMPOSITION. This card's wide rectangular shape evokes the water in a pond or tank, a suitable universe for the dimly seen school of fish.

RHYTHM AND REPETITION. Schooling fish move together, and so do these monochromatic images of fish layered on top of one another. This is a good example of artful repetition with underlying syncopation that's not necessarily rhythmic.

LINE. There is no more evocative line than that created by a Chinese lettering brush in a skilled hand. Each character flows into the next in a way that suggests harmony and life. The sharpness of the brushwork brings the writing into the foreground, while the fish recede into the murky background.

By partially inking a stamp of a single fish, the artist has been able to create the impression of a school of fish dimly seen beneath the surface of a pond—a superb design with only a single stamp.

COLOR. The simplicity of adding harmonious yellow and blue color to one fish, while the rest remain an indistinct brown, makes this card a window into the water. The faded color of the background fish adds great depth to the illusion.

CONTEXT. In Chinese art a school of fish represents prosperity and abundance. While we don't know what the Chinese characters say, we can expect this card to carry a thank you or some other piece of good news.

GET A LIFT
FROM GOOD COMPOSITION

CONTEXT. Balloons always express happiness and usually are associated with a party. This party invitation invites the recipient to lift the flap and enjoy the message inside.

COMPOSITION. At first glance there's nothing symmetrical or balanced about this composition. But actually, the line of symmetry is the diagonal from upper left to lower right. The strong diagonal line helps the balloons lift into the air.

RHYTHM AND REPETITION. The card repeats the three balloon shapes, which were made by stamping, then punching. Like a stamp, a punch makes the same shape every time, helping to unify the design. The rhythmic background is like the beat in music—it ties everything together without intruding.

LINE. The lines that connect the balloons to the ribbon aren't drawn or stamped at all— they're made from fine gold thread. Use your imagination to devise ways to create an expressive line.

COLOR. The designer has chosen a yellow-gold palette of closely related colors. This is the simplest way to guarantee color harmony.

In this symmetrical composition, the symmetry balances across a diagonal line. Approached creatively, symmetry doesn't have to be mechanical.

TIP

When you want to stamp an image onto a punched cutout, stamp first, then punch. It's easy to align the image in the punch, but very difficult to stamp in exactly the right place on something that's already been punched out.

FOUR SQUARES

COMPOSITION. Although the background card is a rectangle, the black square dominates. The card is a square, the four motifs fit within squares. Each leafy rosette has been worked within a circle that almost fills the square. You'll never go wrong by choosing a basic shape and repeating it.

RHYTHM AND REPETITION. The four motifs, though very similar, are not identical. And although three of them are arranged in a regular pattern, the fourth slides off the page. Clearly the artist has deliberately broken away from precise patterning, but why? The formal composition becomes informal, inviting the recipient to investigate further, open it up, see what it might say.

LINE. Varying the weight and quality of lines can suggest depth and shadow. For the best illusion of depth, imagine the direction of the light and manipulate the line weights accordingly.

COLOR. Monochromatic color schemes not only convey a feeling of calm and harmony, they are not at all complicated. All you need to do is choose a color you like, see what shades and hues you can make of it, and stay with that limited palette.

CONTEXT. Maybe these rosettes are carved wood, maybe they are tooled leather. The motifs represent natural leaves and plants, and while their arrangement around a center suggests a more formal era, the tilting squares make it contemporary.

This four-square composition could have been boring, until the artist tipped the fourth square off the page.

TIP

By definition, the sides of a square are the same length—that is, their proportion is 1-to-1. When a card is twice as high as it is wide, its proportions are 2-to-1. The ancient Greeks discovered the Golden Rectangle, whose proportions are 1.62-to-1. When you divide a square off a Golden Rectangle, the shape that remains is another Golden Rectangle. No other shape has this property. When asked to choose a card with the most pleasing proportions, most people will select something very close to a Golden Rectangle.

These formally composed cards illustrate the value of simple color harmonies and proportions. Above, the circles sit within a square inside another square—basic shapes that have no up or down. At right, all the rectangles are about the same shape. When in doubt, simplify.

H aving reviewed all these designs, when all is said and done, there's one thing that is more important than any list of elements. This is your personal message and your feelings about it. Whenever you get tangled up in design rules and guidelines, it's easy to lose sight of your message and even why you are making the card in the first place. But when you work with the design elements keeping your message clearly in mind, your success is guaranteed.

If achieving color harmony baffles you, stick with simple palettes of closely related colors. Try working with shades and hues of a single color, or with two colors that appear next to one another on the color wheel.

SIMPLE STAMPING

Even the least sophisticated stamping techniques can yield elegant, whimsical, artistic, playful—even glamorous—results. None of the techniques in this chapter are at all difficult; some are starkly simple, and some look complicated, but perhaps only because of the addition of an extra element—an eyelet, a ribbon, or a trinket. Small finishing touches can add interesting detail and produce very polished-looking projects. Don't think for a moment that your horizons are limited because you don't own everything that's for sale at the stamp store. It's all up to you and your willingness to make the most of your materials. Play with the materials you have on hand and try using them in different ways. Experiment! You can launch plenty of interesting and impressive designs with just a few stamps, black ink, and a small palette of colors. Try stamping an image in black and then in various colors on various types of paper to get an idea of the different effects at your fingertips.

A handful of simple techniques, as shown in this chapter, will get you started producing stunning rubber-stamped projects. Repeat stamping—the repetition of an image to create patterns, borders, or clusters of images—and over-stamping—stamping an image once and stamping it again so that part of the second image covers part of the first—are two easy methods that can add variety to any project. And masking, in which parts of a stamped project are "masked" out, is used by both new and veteran stampers alike with great results. If there is one technique (and concept) we would like to see you master at the outset it would be this one. You can mask the stamped image to prevent over-stamping it or you can mask around the image to keep the background clean. See the information about masks in the Basic Stamping chapter. Discovering simple variations on these basic methods for yourself, whether it be through trial and error or just through an attempt to try something new, provides some of stamping's most satisfying moments.

Simple stamping combined with a basic repertoire of image-making and card-building techniques helps you create an infinite variety of effects. These projects feature repeats, block stamps, and layered paper.

SIMPLE STAMPING

Y ou can stamp different images one atop another to create an extraordinarily rich layered effect. Block stamps are easy to manipulate and can be used to good advantage in stamped artworks to create both stylish backgrounds and foreground images. Some block stamps create simple square, rectangular, and oval spaces, which can either be left as is for a strong graphic statement, over-stamped with one or more images, or artistically combined to create a totally new image.

Thanks for being you

LEANING LEAVES

Over-stamping is a great way to add interest to a card, plus it lets you create fascinating designs with just a single stamp. Depending on how you arrange the images, you have the opportunity to create an unexpected visual twist. The gold edging on the ribbon with these leaves echoes the glow of the metallic inks.

CREATING THE PROJECT
1. Stamp the leaves, slightly overlapping them.
2. Stamp the greeting.
3. Punch two small holes on the card fold about one inch apart, thread the ribbon through, and tie a bow.

TIP

O verlaying one image on another is best done with a simple design. Let the single image take centerstage.

LAYERED COLORS
The addition of a block stamped as the bottom image here adds an extra element. It's almost like putting the main image onstage. These beautiful, subtle leaf images were created by layering two colors of ink.

PERFECT PRESENTS by Autumn Koepp

Masking can be used in all sorts of situations, from stamping a series of background images right up to the central image, to stamping images one in front of another to create a scene with a distinct foreground and background, to defining the shape of the image while keeping the background clear. Here two block stamps were stacked to make an inviting pile of presents. Dot and flower stamps create the wrapping paper. The flower stamp we used to decorate the wrapping paper was actually larger than the present, but a mortise mask helped contain the stamped decoration within the blocks. A pretty ribbon slipped through slits at the top and bottom of the stack ties up the bundle.

CREATING THE PROJECT

1. Ink and stamp the blocks in aqua on white cardstock.
2. Mask off the outside of the blocks. With sky blue ink, stamp dots on the top box, and flowers and dots on the bottom one.
3. Cut a slit at the top and bottom of the pile, pull through the blue organdy ribbon, and tie a bow.
4. Layer on dark cardstock to frame the image and then place onto the card.

AUTUMN PLACE CARD

A mask made from the single leaf stamped onto paper and then silhouetted covers the first stamped leaf (the one in the foreground) so that the other two leaves, when stamped, miraculously take their places behind the featured player.

CREATING THE PROJECT

1. Stamp the leaf with its stem in the lower corner of a place card.
2. Make a mask of the leaf by stamping it onto lightweight paper and then cutting it out, removing the stem.
3. Place the mask over the stamped leaf and stamp the remaining two leaves so that they overlap the mask.
4. Remove the mask to reveal the layered leaves.

thinking of you

FLOWERED BLOCK by Kathy Perkins

Use a mortise mask to keep the background clear of stamped images or stray ink, especially when you want to place images on top of but partially off the edge of the underlying stamped image. This repeatedly stamped little flower over a swirly block stamp has been contained to the "live" area (the space inside the cut-out shape) with the use of a mortise mask, resulting in a charming country feeling of windblown flowers.

CREATING THE PROJECT

1. Stamp the block in the center of a small square of white paper cut to frame the center block with about 1/4 inch of white space.
2. Mask around the block to preserve the image and repeatedly stamp the flower over the block design extending it over the mask.
3. Remove the mask and mount the stamped block on the card.
4. Stamp the message below the block.

COFFEE TIME by Kathy Perkins

Simple block images make a strong statement when stamped in contrasting colors. Although the two side blocks here look like they have been created using the same technique as the card opposite, they are in fact a block stamp with the design (cup) image depressed rather than raised. The middle cup is actually a single image stamped over a block.

CREATING THE PROJECT

1. Stamp an empty block in the center of a rectangular piece of cardstock.
2. Stamp a block with a cup on each side.
3. Stamp a cup onto the center block.
4. Layer onto a card.

BUTTERFLIES IN FLIGHT

by Autumn Koepp

Try experimenting and you'll find that the same outline stamp that produces a positive image when inked and pressed to paper can create a negative image on paper when pressed uninked against the inked block stamp itself. Pressing the uninked stamp against the inked block stamp removes some of the ink prior to stamping on paper. By using this technique you can get two completely different effects with one stamp. In this card, carefully placing the butterflies in a different position on each block creates a feeling of spontaneous flight when the three blocks are completed.

CREATING THE PROJECT

1. Ink the block stamp with pigment ink and before it dries press the butterfly stamp against it to remove some of the ink.
2. Stamp the block on paper to reveal a color block containing the "un-inked" butterfly image.
3. Clean both stamps and repeat the process twice, moving the butterfly on the block each time to simulate flight once all three are finished.
4. Stamp the greeting in pigment ink across the three blocks.

WINTER GREEN by Lara Zazzi

Another use of block stamps, these three freeform rectangles overlap each other as do the trees stamped over the blocks. The resulting natural "forest" captures the look of sunlight filtering through the trees.

CREATING THE PROJECT

1. Stamp the three block rectangle shapes overlapping one another in metallic gold.
2. Stamp the trees, one per block, also overlapping one another, over the gold with moss green ink.
3. Stamp the greeting.
4. Mount on yellow cardstock (to highlight the sunlight).
5. Layer onto warm red cardstock leaving a generous margin.

LET IT SNOW by Lara Zazzi

This effective artwork is accomplished simply with two layers of paper and one of pigment ink atop which the snowflake rests. The soft white block is actually white pigment ink. The pigment ink leaves an opaque, filmy window of color through which we can view the tan cardstock beneath. The dark cardstock as the bottom layer provides a definite ground for the floating snowflake.

CHRISTMAS ORNAMENT CARD by Lara Zazzi

This card is fun, festive, sophisticated, and a snap to make during the busy holiday season. The background is formed with a block stamp; the pretty ornament and bow are created with two colors of pigment ink on a single stamp.

═══

CREATING THE PROJECT

1. Stamp the block stamp on cardstock.
2. Ink the stamp with your colors. Cat's-eye stamps work well because they're easy to manipulate.
3. Stamp over the block.
4. Stamp the greeting.
5. Layer and mount to form the card.

═══

SNAZZY SNOWMAN by Lara Zazzi

This simple card packs a lively punch thanks to the liberal use of glitter.

═══

CREATING THE PROJECT

1. Stamp the block stamp in pale blue ink on cardstock.
2. Using navy blue pigment ink, stamp the snowman over the block. Apply glue and glitter.
3. Stamp the greeting.
4. Layer to form a card.

═══

A WOODLAND SCENE

Using one stamp and one color ink can produce striking results. Some stamps contain incredible detail, like this woodland stamp, and require nothing more for maximum impact than artful layering on special papers and perhaps some simple background stamping. The light brown paper enhances the dark image while the corrugated paper adds a depth and texture to balance the smooth black frame.

CREATING THE PROJECT

1. Stamp the image on tan cardstock.
2. Mount on corrugated paper slightly larger than the cardstock.
3. Assemble the layers onto black cardstock leaving a border equal to the corrugated border.

VARIATIONS ON A THEME

The same stamp used with different colors and different color applications or techniques will produce very different results. The very soft-colored card shown left, was created by coloring on the stamp with daubers and then stamping on ivory paper. The card at far right was stamped with black ink and then finished with colored pencil. One stamp, a few coloring tools, and some interesting papers are all you need to create elegant cards.

LIGHT ON DARK

Once again, a single stamp with single color provides dramatic results, proving that less really is more. Because it's opaque, light pigment ink makes a strong statement on dark paper, creating a perfectly beautiful treatment for this large, etching-style stamp.

CREATING THE PROJECT

1. Stamp the image with light blue metallic ink on black paper.
2. Cut along the outside edge and mount on a contrasting paper to frame.
3. Mount the framed image on a black card to complete.

DRAGONFLY'S PATH

One stamp and one color take simple stamping to the next level. We stamped the image with a dye ink and painted the flower with opaque pigment inks. The slow-drying pigment ink allows you to blend colors to achieve a realistic effect, and because it is opaque the colors are vibrant and gloriously alive. In this project, the background of the flower stamp was cut away to create a window revealing a colorful interior.

CREATING THE PROJECT

1. Stamp the flower with its frame and cut away the background leaving the flower attached where it touches the frame.
2. Glue a printed paper to the inside of the card so that it is visible through the front window when the card is closed.
3. Paint the flower with re-inking ink. Your paintbrush should be wet, but not dripping. Too much water will speed up drying and the paint won't be as opaque.
4. Punch a dragonfly out of the printed paper used for the card interior, and mount it to the card with mounting tape. Pinch the wings up to create some dimension.
5. Draw the dragonfly's flight pattern with dashes.

A FLOCK OF LITTLE GIRLS

It's always satisfying to get lots of use from a stamp. Here we have used a form of paper-layering to create a finished, custom appearance. In this technique, which we are calling double-stamping, you stamp a single image on two different pieces of paper. Then you cut out a part of the second image and glue it to the first image. These cards are a graphic illustration of the many possibilities available with this simple, quick technique. As a bonus, when you use this process, you'll no doubt use up some of those interesting paper scraps you just couldn't throw away.

Our little girl's dress was changed from plain to polka-dot by stamping a second image on printed paper, cutting it out, and overlaying it on the first image. Snazzy glued-on ornaments give the girl personality and pizzazz.

CREATING THE PROJECT

1. Stamp the girl on both cardstock and printed paper.
2. Cut the dress from the printed paper to the inside of the stamped lines. This will allow the dress to fit comfortably within the outline stamped on the card. Glue the dress to the card.
3. Color in the girl's hair, skin, cheeks, and shoes, and glue on the bow, bracelet, and sash.
4. Stamp the greeting using a stamp positioner to keep it straight.
5. Trim the cardstock with deckle-edge scissors and layer to form a card.

VARIATIONS ON A THEME

This card can be infinitely customized. The letter carrier's hair combines black and brown liquid appliqué for a sun-kissed look. The trick-or-treater's patent leather shoes get their shine from dimensional adhesive. She has a button for a hat, while punched pieces create her belt and a black cat.

DUCK, DUCK, DUCK

Stamping an image repeatedly on a card or page can produce a pleasingly rhythmic effect whether you use the technique to make images meander gracefully across a page or march straight across the paper, like our row of little yellow ducks. We used two contrasting printed text-weight papers glued to cardstock to construct this card. For added fun, our ducks float above the card on small pieces of mounting tape.

CREATING THE PROJECT

1. Cut the coordinating papers (these are printed text-weight papers) and attach them to cardstock with spray adhesive.
2. Punch holes for the ribbon and tie the bow.
3. Stamp the ducks and color them in. Cut them out, glue to small squares of sponge, and mount on the card.

BABY CARD

Owning a set of alphabet stamps offers many possibilities. Think of them—personalized stationery, cards, and envelopes for yourself or friends and family, handsome book plates, monogrammed napkins! This card to congratulate the recipient on the birth of a new baby is simple to create yet is both inviting and elegant.

PAPER

*P*aper is as important a material to rubber stamps as images and color. The carnival of colors, textures, and patterns available can be exhilarating. Through trial and error try samples of paper before purchasing a large quantity. Experiment first; see what you like and what works best for you. Let your likes and dislikes be your guide as you try different combinations of papers, stamps, and inks. You'll be surprised at how effectively your experiments will hone your sense of design, and it's almost certain you'll produce some very usable ideas for current and future projects in the process.

There's no one best paper for stamping, since all papers accept inks differently. You will find your own personal favorite combinations among the variety of materials you will need, but it's likely that cardstock will quickly become your workhorse. Cardstock is available in a myriad of sizes, patterns, colors, and surfaces. Easy to use, uncoated cardstock works with all inks. Text papers, which are lighter than cardstock, come in a variety of stationery-appropriate weights so you can customize your own writing paper. Text papers are also perfect for layering and making envelopes. Vellum, a lovely translucent paper, can be put to work in your projects in a number of interesting ways. Beautiful, tactile specialty papers can easily be the focus of a stamped project—think of corrugated cardboard, mylar, and tissue paper. If you're going to be working with watercolors, use watercolor paper. It's made to handle all the water you need to use without ripping or tearing through. And don't forget the plain paper that you probably already have somewhere around your home. Brown paper bags, plain bond paper, butcher paper, and junk mailings all are excellent—and inexpensive—stamping surfaces.

From simple cardstock to translucent vellum, paper is the foundation of most stamping projects. Choose the colors and textures you like, and try to look beyond the obvious. You can stamp on printed papers, gift wrap, corrugated paper, even selected pieces of junk mail. A torn or deckle-cut edge softens the transition from one type of paper to another.

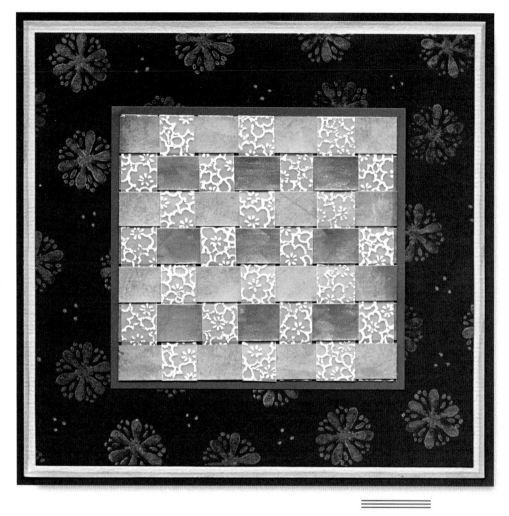

ecause vellum is see-through, you can stamp it from either side to create different and unusual effects; because it's lightweight, you can attach it to heavier papers to create interesting interactions. It's a challenge to attach vellum to cardstock due to the vellum's translucency. We usually attach the vellum with ribbon or an eyelet to maintain a freedom of movement.

PAPER WEAVING

A lovely effect comes from weaving strips of text paper and vellum. You can create cards to feature the weaving, or use the weaving to accent one or more stamped images. In this project, we have woven strips of text paper and vellum independently and attached the weaving to the card as a finished layer. The deep rich color tones in this card come from a mixture of soft iridescent violet, pink, blue, yellow, and green paints, and stamped and embossed vellum.

CREATING THE PROJECT

1. Prepare three pieces of paper for weaving. Use cardstock for the first piece. Spread three colors of acrylic paint, one at a time, in stripes over the cardstock, overlapping the colors—blue, amethyst, and jade were used here. Dab gold over the top with a sponge or a scrunched piece of plastic wrap.
2. The second piece of weaving paper is also cardstock. Coat it with a thin layer of gold paint.
3. For the third piece of weaving paper, use vellum stamped with a floral background stamp and embossed with white embossing powder.
4. When dry, cut all three pieces of paper into 1/2-inch strips and weave. When complete, attach a sheet of double-stick mounting adhesive to the back. Trim into a pleasing square or rectangle, remove the liner on the adhesive backing, and mount on contrasting cardstock.
5. Create the background paper by sponging the same colors of paint onto a floral design stamp and randomly stamping. Add clusters of gold dots using the point of a wooden skewer or a gold paint pen.
6. Sponge along the edge with gold paint.
7. Layer to form a card.

BEACH PARTY

Vellum is one paper that goes anywhere and does anything—it's just as appropriate on an informal beach-party invitation as it is on cards with a more formal flair. The combination of formal vellum with the casual brown paper here may have seemed illogical to the mind, but the eye says it's just right. The vellum complements the toasted marshmallow while adding just a bit of sophistication to the message.

CREATING THE PROJECT

1. Stamp the marshmallow on tan cardstock with archival ink and trim with a deckle-edge scissors.
2. Cut a slit under the stick and marshmallow, starting and stopping 1/4 inch from each side of the card.
3. Print the invitation on medium-weight (#28) vellum. This one was generated by computer, a fast process that insures accuracy over the entire run of invitations.
4. Apply liquid appliqué sparingly on the inside of the marshmallow. After the liquid appliqué has set overnight, puff it up by heating the paper from underneath with a heat gun. Use tan chalk to "toast" the edges.
5. Trim and insert the vellum in the slit in the cardstock and secure.
6. Mount on blue cardstock.

TIP

Spend your time on the fun part of stamping. Write the invitation once and copy it onto vellum. Or use your computer to print on the vellum. It's faster and more accurate!

Please join
John and Jennifer
for a picnic on the beach
Friday, July 14th, 6:30
140 Pilots Point
R.s.v.p. 203 221-1229

STATIONERY

You can do some nice things with lightly patterned text papers—often only a single stamp or a simple stamped border at the top of the paper is enough to set your stationery apart from commercial offerings. Of course you can also stamp a border along one side of the paper or a cluster of images in the center if this better suits your taste. The back of stationery paper is a blank canvas, and if you typically write short notes, you might want to stamp the back with a matching pattern, since it gives the stationery a pretty, finished look when folded.

ASIAN IRIS

Basic cardstock is off-white and white. But many texture variations are offered—linen, woven, ribbed, flat, etc. Smooth cardstock is the best choice when you are working with fine, detailed stamps. Try creating your own patterned background paper to balance the main image.

CREATING THE PROJECT

1. Generously ink the stamp with gold metallic ink. With the rubber side of the stamp up, dab on various colors of pigment ink from a dauber over the top of the gold to highlight the irises. Apply extra pressure when you stamp because you have two layers of ink on most of the stamp.
2. Ink the greeting and stamp.
3. Repeatedly ink and stamp the design in a complementary color to create a background paper.
4. Layer to form a card.
5. Adorn with a Chinese "Good Luck" coin.

HAPPY BIRTHDAY

These quilt-like squares punched or cut from textured paper add dimensional interest, particularly against the soft linen finish of the ivory stock beneath it. The subtle greeting, stamped in watermark ink, echoes the smoothness of the base cardstock.

CREATING THE PROJECT

1. Punch or cut out nine squares; assemble them in the shape of a gift box.
2. Attach a ribbon bow at the top.
3. Stamp the greeting below the gift on the background paper.

SWINGING VIOLETS
by Kathy Perkins

Attaching the vellum to the cardstock takes a new angle. Here the eyelet holds the stamped vellum square to the card while allowing freedom to swing to and from its block stamped base.

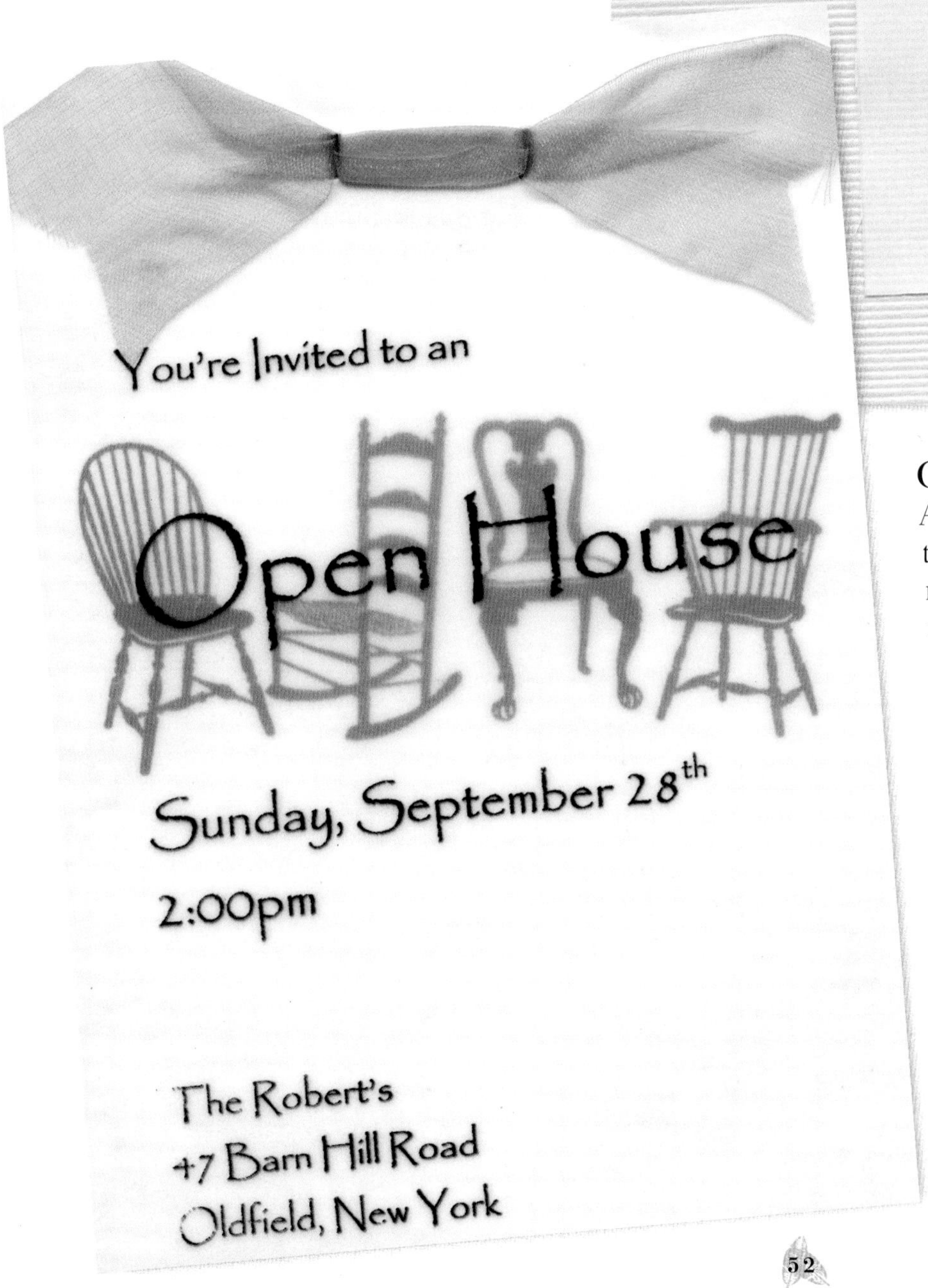

You're Invited to an

Open House

Sunday, September 28th

2:00pm

The Robert's
47 Barn Hill Road
Oldfield, New York

OPEN HOUSE
A printed vellum overlay suits this homespun invitation perfectly. The translucency of the vellum makes the wood chairs appear soft and welcoming, and supports the crisp black computer-generated old-style lettering. The wood-tone bow adds a shot of color.

CREATING THE PROJECT
1. Using a computer, compose and print out your invitations on vellum.
2. Stamp the image with four chairs on card.
3. Attach the vellum to the cardstock by punching two holes about an inch apart near the top and in the center of both the vellum and cardstock. Insert the ribbon through both holes from the top, cross in the back, and bring up through the holes.

FLIGHT OF THE BUTTERFLIES by Marg Hjelmstad

This project uses vellum fragments arranged to promote the feeling of motion and flight. The tiny piece in the corner accentuates the colored butterfly, making it seem closer at hand.

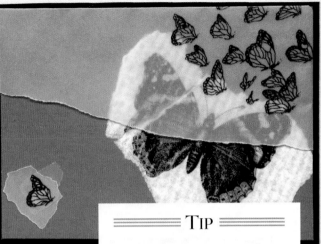

CREATING THE PROJECT

1. Stamp the largest butterfly onto thin white paper using black ink. Add color with markers. Tear the image roughly to shape.
2. Tear off a section of wing and reassemble if desired.
3. Stamp the smaller butterflies onto lightweight vellum. Tear as desired and wrap around the cardstock, taping in back.
4. Stamp and color a single butterfly on vellum, tear as desired, and mount on the cardstock. Here the butterfly was mounted on an underlayer of torn vellum to intensify the color. Layer and mount to a card.

GRAZING COW by Marg Hjelmstad

In this card, a tranquil country scene is given a fragile, misty look thanks to a vellum layer. The foreground tree that has been stamped on the front and colored on the reverse side adds a pleasant—and surprising—sense of dimension.

CREATING THE PROJECT

1. Stamp the house on cardstock. Stamp a bare tree on each side. Mask the upper trunks of both trees and stamp the evergreens behind. Stamp fence posts of various sizes in the foreground so they appear to recede. Mask the first two posts and stamp the cow.
2. Color the images and, using grass-tuft stamps, fill in the pasture.
3. Hand-draw the barbed wire.
4. On a sheet of vellum, stamp the largest tree in black dye ink and color with marker on the reverse side.
5. Wrap the vellum around the cardstock so that the top of the tree is correctly positioned; fasten in back with tape.
6. Layer to form a card.

TIP

Torn paper is one of our favorite effects. Vellum is especially easy to tear and leaves a pleasing, soft edge. You can vary the feathering of the edge by the direction in which you tear the paper—either toward or away from you.

MUSICAL MOMENT by Ann Zazzi

Don't think you have to tiptoe around vellum. Despite its ethereal look, vellum isn't particularly fragile—you can even use it to make boxes. Because the surface of vellum is coated, it means it won't absorb ink. Therefore, as with matte-coated cardstock, if you're going to use pigment ink with vellum emboss the ink to make it permanent. Vellum makes a wonderful contribution when used on photo cards. Because you can stamp and emboss it, you can have fun combining images with your featured photo—it's a little like creating a double exposure with a camera. In this case, the music stamp sets the tone of the card while the winsome musician playfully peeks out.

CREATING THE PROJECT

1. Stamp the music on vellum in clear embossing ink and emboss with opaque white.
2. Place the vellum over a photo that has been layered onto a card.
3. Secure the vellum to the card with ribbon.

TIP

Although vellum is not generally fragile, it does need careful attention when you are embossing it. Preheat the heat tool and then emboss quickly to avoid overheating and therefore curling the vellum.

GLAD PLAID by Kim Smith

Vellum is the perfect base for plaid. Because it's see-through, you can color on both sides: here the clear letters of the greeting, stamped on the front of the vellum, blend harmoniously with the soft pattern of color beneath.

CREATING THE PROJECT

1. For the plaid, pull a green ink pad along the length of the underside of the vellum, leaving 1 1/2-inches between stripes. Blot the color on a clean piece of paper, and repeat with the same pad in the opposite direction. Blot again.
2. With the edge of another ink pad, draw horizontal lines across the underside of the paper and blot.
3. Draw vertical lines with yet another ink pad and blot.
4. Stamp the greeting on the front of the vellum.
5. To fasten the ribbon, insert it through two punched holes from the front, cross the ribbon in back, and bring back to the front through the same holes.

TIP

Remember when using pigment ink on glossy paper you must emboss to make it permanent.

ILLUMINATED INKWELL NOTE CARD by Joyce Hazen

The inkwell and pen, one area of a larger stamp, were stamped with dye ink on glossy paper, cropped from the larger image after stamping, and attached to cardstock with photo corners. The contrasting dark-colored uncoated textured paper sandwiched between the glossy stocks accentuates the difference between the two.

CREATING THE PROJECT

1. Apply ink to the stamp with brush markers, lightest color first. Blend colors with a stippling brush before stamping.
2. Stamp onto coated paper.
3. Crop the inkwell and pen portion of the stamp and mount on contrasting matte cardstock with photo corners. Layer on glossy cardstock.

WELL-LOVED BEAR

Art and specialty papers are beautiful and tactile and easily enhance a design. Highly textured art papers are typically used for layering and embellishment or in collage projects rather than as the primary stamping surface, but there is no reason to limit your horizons. If you want to stamp a piece of art on specialty paper, do so. Stamping on textured paper, such as these corrugations, always makes for interesting results, sometimes when you least expect them. Here the stamped bear is supported by contrasting-colored deeply ribbed corrugated stock. The contrast in textures is appealing, and so are the connections. When we stamped the hearts on the red corrugated paper it inspired us to go back and emphasize the corduroy on the bear's feet and hands.

CREATING THE PROJECT

1. Stamp the bear in black on cream cardstock and add color.
2. Trim the cardstock with deckle-edge scissors and highlight the edges by drawing them through a metallic gold pad. There are several ways to create a gold-edged card. Drawing the card across a metallic ink pad produces a rich, soft textured look; drawing along the edge of the card with a gold paint pen provides a cleaner, straighter, brighter solid color.
3. Randomly stamp the heart in gold metallic ink on the red corrugated paper.
4. Assemble the card.
5. Layer on tan cardstock.

TIP

The texture of the paper and the dimension of the stamp help determine the appropriate size of the mat supporting the main image. Our well-loved bear is surrounded by a mat wide enough to accommodate a good-sized heart stamp, which itself is large enough to balance the substantial rib of the corrugated paper.

MAKE MINE MYLAR

Mylar is fun and glitzy and can be layered just like any other paper. When used underneath cardstock with punched cutouts, it adds sparkling dimension to a design. Here the mylar provides a glistening border and some of the balloon shapes, making them appear as light as air.

CREATING THE PROJECT

1. Stamp the dancers near the bottom of your cardstock, leaving plenty of room for the balloons. Color with markers. Color the dots on the dancers' pants with a fine-tip silver metallic paint pen.
2. Punch out balloons from scraps of mylar and coordinating cardstock and glue them to the card.
3. Draw the balloon strings with a fine-tip black pen.
4. Layer on mylar and then dark cardstock to finish.

PLAYFUL POOCH

Most stampers experiment with watercolors at some point because of the lovely, blended effects they can produce. This cute hound owes the lifelike gradations of his coat color to watercoloring with brush markers. The punched dog bones glued in the corner focus all eyes on man's best friend.

CREATING THE PROJECT

1. Ink the stamp using a brown brush marker and stamp on watercolor paper.
2. With a wet paintbrush, "pull" the ink to feather out the color. Color the scarf with yellow marker.
3. Draw a line under the dog with a light gray brush marker and pull with a wet paintbrush.
4. Layer with yellow cardstock and mount on the card.
5. Frame with punched-out dog bones in the corners.

TIP

Treat open space—blank white watercolor paper—as another color. Don't feel obliged to cover the whole surface with color.

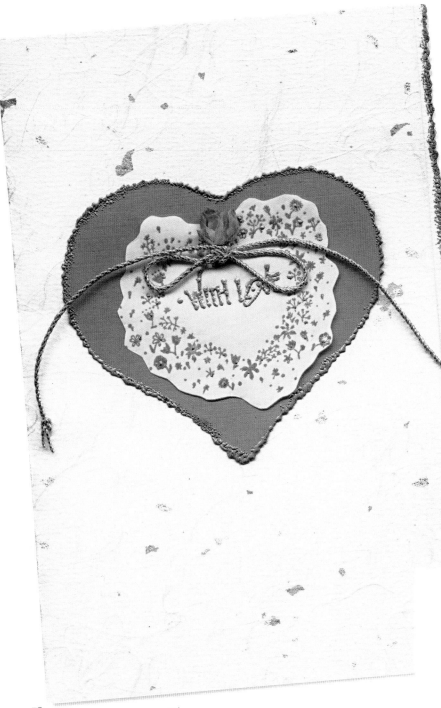

WEDDING GREETINGS

Special papers can be so sumptuous that you need little else to create a beautiful card. The paper used here provides the perfect background for a straightforward message of love for a wedding day.

CREATING THE PROJECT

1. Attach decorative paper to cardstock to form a card. Trim front edge to reveal a decorative embossed edge on the inside page of the card.

2. Using a stencil, cut a heart shape with a deckle-edge scissors.

3. Outline the heart edge with an embossing pen. Emboss in gold.

4. Stamp the field of small flowers on parchment paper and trim to a loose heart shape.

5. Stamp and emboss the greeting in the center of the parchment heart.

6. Tie the parchment heart to the larger cardstock heart with a cord and embellish with a dried rose.

7. Glue to the card.

VARIATION ON A THEME

This red heart, cut from red vellum, sits beautifully on a swirled block image stamped in metallic. The color and texture of the smooth red vellum balance the uneven tones of the neutral color beneath. The heart is predominant although the understamping is clearly visible.

LEAVES AND BAMBOO by Frankie Fioretti

Resist paper is another specialty paper well worth incorporating into your repertoire. These papers are manufactured with an embedded design treated with a special ink. As you apply ink to the paper, the design will surface, as different areas of the paper will absorb the ink in different ways. An artful combination of leaf-patterned resist paper and sponge technique results in an artwork of unparalleled richness. The artist has balanced color, shape, form, texture, and dimension in a most appealing way.

CREATING THE PROJECT

1. To create the background, lightly sponge the paper with iridescent ink. Stamp with the bamboo stamp repeatedly using metallic gold ink.

2. On the leaf-resist paper, sponge a heavier coat of the iridescent ink used for the background. Tear the edges and sponge with iridescent gold ink. Layer onto black cardstock leaving a narrow mat.

3. For the next layer, use a coarser sponge to create a mottled appearance.

4. Color layer four with a wad of scrunched-up plastic wrap. When dry, cut into shapes that lend interest to the overall design.

5. The central image is layered onto black cardstock. To create the central design, sponge on the background color and spritz with water. Squeeze metallic gold ink in a freeform shape of your choice onto a flat compressed sponge and stamp the sponge onto the background.

6. Assemble the layers and mount on a card.

COLOR

Color brings life to rubber-stamp art. Color conveys feelings and emotions. Color is exciting. Whether you choose to feature a simple color scheme or a kaleidoscope of hues, you're bound to have fun bringing your ideas to life with color. Understanding how colors work together will increase your design confidence, keep your projects on track, and save you from squandering money on inks and paints that may be lovely but are not consistent with the artwork you wish to make.

You probably remember the color wheel from school. It's simply the rainbow arranged as a circular diagram, so it shows the relationships between colors. The rainbow contains red, orange, yellow, green, blue, and violet, and they march around the wheel in that order. When you add black to a color, the result is called a shade: blue-black is a shade of blue. When you add white to a color, it's called a hue: pink is a hue of red. Colors that are next to one another, like green and blue, are called adjacent or analogous. Colors that appear across from one another, like green and red, are called complementary. For any two colors, there's a third color that contains them both: red and yellow can be said to meet together in orange. Sets of three colors that meet in this way are called triads.

When you want to send a calm message, it's best to stay with shades and hues of a single color (a monochromatic color scheme). When you add a second color, the composition is likely to be calmer if you stick with shades and hues of an analogous pair. To make the composition more lively and exciting, go across the color wheel for the complementary color, or try working with a triad of three colors.

Color adds life to a project, and colors that are well-chosen harmonize together like music. You can see in these examples the use of monochromatic color schemes, complementary and adjacent colors, and color triads. When you put colors together, it's important to harmonize their intensity as well as the color values themselves: put muted colors together, or strong colors together. When you mix colors of different intensities, you may create a jangling effect—which might be just what your project needs.

COLOR

C olor, paper texture, and form offer an incredible range of design choices to the stamper willing to experiment. Being able to use pieces of one stamp creatively gives you access to a wide range of possibilities. The three projects on this spread are a wonderful exercise in developing your creativity. We have used one stamp to create three very different looks. The stamp itself is actually the black outline as seen here. Look what the application of color and the interesting play of parts of the stamp can do. The dramatic dark purple glitter under the window plastic offers a sophisticated view of the natural world. Another version is silhouetted with a drawn watercolored leaf and stem. Another silhouettes three flowers with one framed in a window. The colors are simple and effective.

DAISY 1

This card, though fairly simple to create, is a study in sophisticated contrasts. The bold outline of the daisy is accentuated by dark purple and green opaque glitter and the shine of the window plastic. The layers under the flower are elegant, providing a stark contrast to the central image.

CREATING THE PROJECT

1. Stamp the image on clear window plastic using permanent ink.
2. Cut a piece of double-sided adhesive slightly larger than the flower image, remove one liner, and place the exposed adhesive against the stamped side of the window plastic. Cut out the image.
3. On the liner you removed from the adhesive, stamp the same image using archival ink. Because the liner is coated and will not absorb the ink immediately, blot on scrap paper. This will become your mask, so cut away the part of the image on which you wish to apply background glitter.
4. Remove the liner from the adhesive on the window plastic and replace it with the cutout mask. Apply the background glitter to the exposed adhesive.
5. Remove the mask and apply the second color of glitter. Mount on the background paper and then on the card.

DAISY 2

This bold outline daisy silhouetted and mounted on textured watercolor paper contains delicate yellow petals and contrasts with the soft, freeform green leaf and stem. The green mat trimmed in gold provides a perfect frame against the purple cardstock beneath and the white textured watercolor on top. The colors all work together in presenting a rich look to a well-designed card.

CREATING THE PROJECT

1. Stamp the flower on yellow cardstock and silhouette.
2. Draw the stem and leaf with watercolor on watercolor paper.
3. Paint a base or shadow. Glue the flower atop the stem.
4. Using a mesh brayer with gold metallic ink, stamp the green background panel behind the flower. Edge with a gold paint pen.
5. Layer on purple cardstock to create a card and attach a pearl button to the daisy center.

DAISY 3

Using the one flower stamp with its frame at the center, two more of the same flowers, silhouetted, dance around the central image.

CREATING THE PROJECT

1. Stamp the whole image three times on white paper.
2. Silhouette two flowers and set aside.
3. Trim around the petals inside the frame leaving the flower attached to its frame.
4. Trim with a deckle-edge scissors around the frame at the flower's outside point. Edge with a silver paint pen.
5. Outline the interior part of each petal with pink paint.
6. Fill in the flower centers with the silver paint pen.
7. Tie the frame to the top of the card and arrange the two silhouetted flowers below it.

GREEN COLLAGE by Gwen Berg

A monochromatic palette can be used effectively in card design. Papers of different colors and textures stamped with the same color ink offer distinct variations on the simple color tones. The torn edges of the paper accept ink differently, providing a darker tone to the green highlights, a dramatic intensity of color.

CREATING THE PROJECT

1. Stamp the text on paper and tear to a pleasing shape.
2. Run a brush marker along the edge to highlight.
3. Stamp the leaves in green and cut into squares.
4. Stamp the background tulips and overstamp with a crackle stamp.
5. The two-faced head is stamped on a dark paper, cut, and mounted.
6. Assemble.

 TIP

We used a stamp with a crackle image to produce this "aged" effect.

AUTUMN LEAVES

Preserve the fleeting beauty of autumn leaves forever with this lovely card. Rainbow pads contain several blocks of colors in one container. Stamp across the color to create lovely effects. In this project we used a brayer to pick up the color from the rainbow pad and apply it to the paper. The ribbon color matches the paper, adding to the central image. The crimps in the leaves create an interesting blend of light and shadow, complementing the rainbow ink used on matte-coated paper.

CREATING THE PROJECT

1. Using a brayer and a dye rainbow pad, apply color to the matte-coated paper. Stamp the oak leaf three times on the brayered paper using black archival ink.
2. Cut out the leaves and run each one through a wave crimper. Vary the direction of the crimp on each leaf for visual interest.
3. Mount the leaves onto cardstock with pieces of foam mounting tape to add dimension. Punch a 1/8-inch hole on each side of the top leaf stem. Insert the ribbon from the back and tie a bow.
4. Cut the second layer of cardstock (the one you are using as a frame) 3/8 inch larger in both directions than the first layer and punch out all four corners with a decorative corner slot punch. The first cardstock slips into the punched slots.
5. Mount on a card.

RAINBOW FISH

One of the beauties of a rainbow ink pad is its simplicity—a lot of color in one impression. The light colors of this rainbow pad are perfect for an "under the sea" card. A clever touch: the little silver fish are cut out with decorative scissors and a facile manipulation.

CREATING THE PROJECT

1. Using a rainbow pad stamp the images.
2. Using paper edgers cut a straight line on the metallic sticker paper.
3. Turn the paper over and trim alongside the first cut, lining up the points so that the little fish shapes appear. Cut and glue in place.
4. Round the corners, layer, and mount on a card.

DEW DROPS by Autumn Koepp

Spritz a block stamp coated with ink just before stamping and you'll produce a random peppering of bubbles. The appearance suggests dew or raindrops—a wonderful background for this elegant flower stamp. The linen-textured paper adds to the effect.

CREATING THE PROJECT

1. Ink the block stamp and spritz with water. Stamp on the linen-textured paper.
2. Ink the flower stamp using pigment ink and stamp with the stem extended below the colored block background.
3. Cut a second color paper, slightly larger than the first, to create a mat.
4. Layer the papers onto a larger card. Instead of using glue to hold the layers together, we tied the project together with an exquisite ribbon.

WATERCOLOR FLOWER by Autumn Koepp

Specialty inks, such as watermark inks, resist inks, and metallic inks, produce great special effects. Watermark inks print a tone-on-tone appearance, creating the illusion of a watermark. Here, adjoining diamonds stamped with watermark ink create a subtle, sophisticated interplay of tones. The purple flower and lavender frame contrast with the green diamonds just as the organic flower contrasts with the geometric background.

CREATING THE PROJECT

1. Ink the flower stamp with markers and stamp on watercolor paper. Blend with a wet paintbrush.
2. Stamp the diamond background with watermark ink.
3. Mount the flower onto lavender stock to frame and position above center on the background.

=== TIP ===

Remember, when working with solid stamps (as in our sample), apply a little extra pressure to make sure all the ink transfers to the paper.

A TRIO OF POLISHED APPLES

Brush markers have several advantages. They give a stamper more control over where the color goes—important in detailed designs. You can use markers to ink a stamp in one or many colors. As an extra plus, the huge assortment of color markers available makes it easy to match paper colors. Solid stamps like these apples require a careful blending of colors to add interest. Because brush markers are so wet they are ideal for this application. The variety of bush marker colors available is wide enough to accommodate any palette. Look at the shine on these apples and the lifelike depth of color accomplished by using coated paper. The gold corrugated mat presents the apples as in a gift box and accentuates the stamped gold swirls on the background.

CREATING THE PROJECT

1. Ink the stamp with brush markers in your favorite apple colors, applying the lightest colors first to create highlights. Surround the light patches with your apple colors. Outline the apple on the bottom and side edges with a darker color marker to create a shadow. Go back with the light colors and blend to "join" the highlights to the apple.
2. When all ink is applied, breathe on the stamp with an open-mouthed "hah" to remoisten the ink.
3. Stamp and emboss gold swirls on the maroon background paper, then layer and mount on a card.

FRAMED MORNING GLORIES

Metallic and extra-metallic inks give projects a glamorous, sophisticated look. When accented with other colors of ink the metallic surface glimmers subtly, without becoming over-powering. Double-inking—a base coat of metallic ink high-lighted with additional metallic colors—creates a sensational blended effect, allowing the base bronze to peek out from beneath the colors. All of this is made easier with the use of ink daubers because of their small-sized ink applicators.

CREATING THE PROJECT

1. Ink the stamp with plenty of bronze metallic ink, then (using daubers) add various metallic colors.
2. Apply extra pressure when stamping with this double layer of ink to achieve a smooth blended effect.
3. Stamp a greeting, if desired, and layer with a comple-mentary color to form a card.

VARIATION ON A THEME

The outline-style morning glories have been created using the same application of metallic inks as the framed morning glories. The nicely stylized greeting here is embossed in gold.

ANTIQUE ROSE

Colored pencils are especially versatile—the colors they produce are soft but vibrant, and since pencil colors can be layered, you can outline or emphasize the details of your artwork to your heart's content. Colored pencils used alone within the confines of an image stamped in rich black ink can produce an eye-catching effect, as the muted colors of the pencils graphically contrast with the outline. Colored pencils are easy to work with. Vary the amount of pressure applied as you color, and see the wonderful difference in tone. Start with a simple project such as this rose where the stamp designer has indicated subtleties like shading and shadows. With the application of color using pencils you enhance the existing shadows/shading without having to master the technique of creating them yourself. The darker shadows are formed by applying more pressure as you color. We usually add a light application of color as a base and then go over the areas, applying more pressure for shading and shadows, using the stamped lines as a guide. The color of the pencil doesn't change, but the amount of pressure applied and the number of layers do. The antique effect of this card was achieved by using a special "antiquing" stamp in light brown ink. The soft deckled edge of the card reinforces the feminine look.

CREATING THE PROJECT

1. Stamp the rose with black ink and color with pencils.
2. Color the antiquing stamp with a marker.
3. Trim the image and outline with a gold paint pen.
4. Layer with contrasting colors to form a card.

TIP

Stamp first on scrap paper to lighten a color, before stamping on your good paper, as we did here with the antiquing stamp. If you have the color you want don't bother with the scrap paper.

BY THE SEA by Dana DeCicco

There is no better way to layer color than with colored pencils. With varying amounts of pressure applied to the strokes, you can truly bring a scene to life by adding texture and color depth. The variations achieved with the build-up of color add some movement to the scene. The paper itself must have some texture ("tooth") to accept the color. The tan paper used here is the perfect base for a coastal scene. This scene was carefully planned ahead of time with six stamps—three of them are rocks! Duplicating the appearance of natural light and ocean water is the challenge here. Black ink, masks, and several stamps were used to create the base of this project.

CREATING THE PROJECT

1. Using a black ink pad, stamp the images to create a coastal scene. Mask as necessary to impart dimension.
2. With colored pencils, layer the colors to create depth and bring the scene to life.
3. Use a blender pencil where colors meet or are layered to soften the effect. Highlight the projected glow on the lighthouse, create the sea foam and rock highlights as well as the light beam and its shadows with white pencil.

SEA SCENE by Frankie Fioretti

You can control visual depth with color: soft hues and deep shades move toward the back, while strong colors advance. The universe of colored and textured papers gives you limitless choices for creating successful paper-layering and collages. This liquid watercolor collage in deep blue/green sea colors evokes the feeling of an underwater scene. The dark blue embossed nautilus shape provides a strong, graphic focal point. Don't feel you have to create this card exactly as it appears here. Use it for inspiration.

CREATING THE PROJECT

1. Paint light blue wash onto white cardstock leaving a small margin around all four sides.
2. Sponge a second piece of white paper with a variety of blue and green watercolor inks.
3. Tear the sponged blue/green paper into three pieces.
4. Construct the card by layering torn pieces of handmade gold paper with the torn blue/green paper.
5. Stamp and emboss the nautilus.
6. Layer onto navy blue cardstock. Add brush strokes of glue across the page to indicate the flow of water. Cover the glue with ultrafine holeless glass beads.

TIP

Experiment with tearing papers. Remember that handmade papers tear differently than machine-made papers. Machine-made papers have a definite grain, which allows for clean tearing in one direction and random, soft tearing in the other. Torn handmade papers offer a random feathered effect when torn in both directions. Before tearing handmade papers paint a line of water where you want to tear. The paper will tear easily along the damp edge.

WATERCOLOR WINTER by Dave Brethauer

The blendability of watercolors means you can create both gorgeous mixtures of color and realistic shadows and shadings in your projects. This project is a good example of selecting colors of inks and papers that are very appropriate to the stamp, in this case to enhance the strong, simple design Note the interesting angles and strong colors and textures of the layers.

CREATING THE PROJECT
1. Stamp the image with black archival ink on watercolor paper.
2. Color the image with watercolors.
3. Create shadows by determining the source of light and how it would affect the objects.
4. Layer papers to create the card.

PANSY CARD

The light acetate butterflies on this card float off the paper. The intensity of the colors is achieved by painting with liquid watercolor ink.

CREATING THE PROJECT
1. Stamp the pansy background on cardstock in black ink and emboss using clear embossing powder. Paint the background with liquid watercolor and edge with a gold paint pen.
2. Sponge a background on another piece of cardstock with a light shade of the colors used in Step 1. Stamp and emboss the greeting in black. Edge with a gold paint pen.
3. Layer the stamped greeting onto two pieces of colored cardstock and mount onto the background.
4. Stamp the butterflies with permanent ink on acetate, color, and apply double-sided adhesive to the back, leaving the second liner intact.
5. Remove the second liner, apply glitter to the adhesive, and face with a second acetate butterfly. Cut out the sandwiched butterflies and attach to the card.

TIP

Blend watercolors as you change colors. Remember to lay down the light colors first.

ROMANCE

A collage is a potpourri of images pasted together to form a two-dimensional work. Where does stamping fit in? Tucked amid all the dried flowers, charms, ribbons, or what-have-you, rubber-stamped words and pictures can tie a project together by serving as a pleasing background; these same words and pictures can also provide unique visual images that stand on their own. This collage, entitled "Romance," features a background of blended paints with gold highlights. In the foreground are a stamped fragment of a faux treasured letter, a stamped table for two, and a luggage tag stamped with X and O kisses and hugs. Romantic, indeed.

CREATING THE PROJECT

1. Create the background by applying various watercolors to the paper. Apply gold highlights with a dry sponge.
2. Stamp the words on the letter fragment with watermark ink. With a dry paintbrush apply dry paint pigment to the paper. Tear to the shape you want, edge with a clear embossing pen, and then emboss with gold powder.
3. Stamp the table and chairs onto lavender mulberry paper. Wet the edges of the paper. This releases thread fragments as you tear the paper. Stamp and emboss the luggage tag.
4. Assemble the collage.

GARDENER'S DELIGHT

The sketchiness of this stamp design mates perfectly with the soft quality imparted by watercolors. The background paper is olive green, and the border overlay is reddish brown—complementary colors on the color wheel. The flowers use these same colors. Which did the designer choose first? The answer is, it doesn't matter. But once you've selected a color palette, try to stick to it.

CREATING THE PROJECT

1. Stamp the image in black archival ink.
2. Scribble color from various brush markers onto a paint palette. Pick up the color with a wet paintbrush and apply to the image.
3. Add bird charm, and layer onto a card.

RADIANT BUTTERFLY by Kay Harley

Masking an image lets you stamp right up to its edges with other images without getting ink on the first image. It's an easy way to add depth to a design. In this card, the random stamping of the little butterflies off the cardstock gives a lively look and promotes a feeling of flight.

CREATING THE PROJECT

1. Stamp the large butterfly with black archival ink.
2. Mask it and stamp the small butterflies right up to the edges.
3. Paint the butterflies with slow-drying pearlescent paint, blending the colors with a slightly wet paintbrush.

TIP

Coordinate the paper colors to the inks and vice versa. It's easier to start with the papers then choose ink colors, mixing them to coordinate.

Tulip Column

Try using ink directly from a bottle of ink (which is also used to re-ink your pigment pad) to obtain strong, vivid colors. Because the pigment ink is slow-drying you have time to blend colors with your brush. With this project we used some of the paper color itself as an accent at the top of the tulip. Use very little water on your brush to keep the intense color.

CREATING THE PROJECT

1. Stamp the image in black on cream cardstock and emboss with clear embossing powder. Paint with the ink used to re-ink pigment pads.
2. Cut out the image and mount on complementary cardstock.
3. Layer to form a card.

Pearly Accents

Many products can be used to accent designs with a delightful shimmer. They come in several formulations, all producing slightly different results, so experiment to find the materials that suit you best. When combined with metallics and watermark ink, the effect is stylized, not gaudy. In this card rhinestones cleverly used at the flower centers catch the light, directing the eye to the classic composition.

CREATING THE PROJECT

1. Stamp the flowers with watermark ink on pink paper.
2. With a dry paintbrush, pick up dry paint pigment and outline the flowers—gently rub off the excess with a dry tissue.
3. Cut out each flower and gently roll the petals over your fingers to give them shape.
4. Attach a tiny piece of mounting tape under the center of each petal. Glue the center of the flower and attach the petals to the card. Layer onto a light cardstock to frame.
5. Layer onto a second pink cardstock. Punch diamond-shaped holes in this layer, as shown, under the flowers. Pull through a ribbon before mounting on the card.

FRAMES AND BACKGROUNDS

Even though a background often frames an image, there is a difference between backgrounds and frames. A frame encloses your stamped images, and the background sets the stage for them by lifting them off the page. Frames and backgrounds enhance a stamped project by focusing all eyes on the central image. Have fun with them. It's your decision to be starkly simple, splendidly showy, or even silly. As you look at the examples in this chapter, take a moment to imagine the images standing alone. This will help you understand the design power of frames and backgrounds.

At what phase in the design process should you think about a project's frame and background? More often than not, the best designs incorporate frames and backgrounds as part of the overall design, not as an afterthought. Backgrounds help stampers create both the visual and emotional components of a card. Many projects use the background substance as their basic structure as well, often layering it with lighter materials chosen for color and texture. Layering the background gives you the choice of stamping images directly on the background material, or of stamping them on paper, cutting them out, and gluing them down.

There are two basic approaches to managing the frame. It can be like a picture frame, where the mat is cut so that the art shows through. The second approach consists of layering the artwork on successively larger pieces of paper, so the artwork is above, not underneath, the frame. Although the differences between the two approaches may seem subtle, the changes in visual depth are real. Using the first method, the frame will look like a window onto the artwork, while with the second method, the artwork will look built up on the frame.

The frame sets off and presents your artwork. It's easy to make a frame by cutting a window in the card, so the image shows through. In many stamped projects, however, while the frame appears to be surrounding the image, it's actually a base layer of paper or card with the smaller image glued on top.

DAISY

Layering papers is the stamper's method of creating backgrounds and frames that elevate the central image above the surface. It's an easy and effective way to focus attention on a design. In this project we have used the same stamp for both the main image and the background. To create a subdued tone for the background that would add dimension and support the main image, we stamped first on scrap paper to reduce the amount of ink on the stamp, before stamping m the card.

CREATING THE PROJECT

1. Stamp the daisy in a warm taupe color on scrap paper, and then without re-inking on cardstock in a random pattern. Stamp the image off the edges of the card to create a sense of a larger picture.

2. Stamp the daisy in black ink on tan cardstock. Color with colored pencils.

3. Trim the stamped, colored central image in a square leaving approximately 1/4 inch on either side and 3/8 inch top and bottom.

4. Layer on three sheets of paper, each cut slightly larger than the next. The darkest color (green here) should be the largest—to set the stage.

5. Stamp and emboss the greeting.

CIRCLES AND SQUARES

When circles are used with square or other geometric windows, the combination makes for interesting contrast. The creative cutting and layering of circles as frames around this butterfly complements the circular shapes within its body.

CREATING THE PROJECT

1. Stamp the butterfly using archival ink on cream cardstock. Paint the image with watercolors.

2. Draw a circle around the butterfly so the wings are outside the line. Cut a circle 1/4 inch beyond the drawn one.

3. Lay the circle with the butterfly on a second piece of

cardstock (a complementary color) and cut a larger circle again leaving a 1/4-inch border.

4. Silhouette the butterfly leaving the wings attached to the circle where they touch it. Cut off the antennae and replace them with wire.

5. Mount on a square window card for the see-through effect.

BREAKING THE ICE

Frames can be cut to any shape and size. The fun of breaking the pattern can result in a frame that is as exhilarating as the scene or image it surrounds. Here's a great example of how an imaginative frame can actively contribute to the message of a card's design. The irregular angles and shapes of the frame punched out of white card-stock and mounted on dark blue accentuates the feel-ing of motion and fun. The skater literally bursts out of the stage you've set.

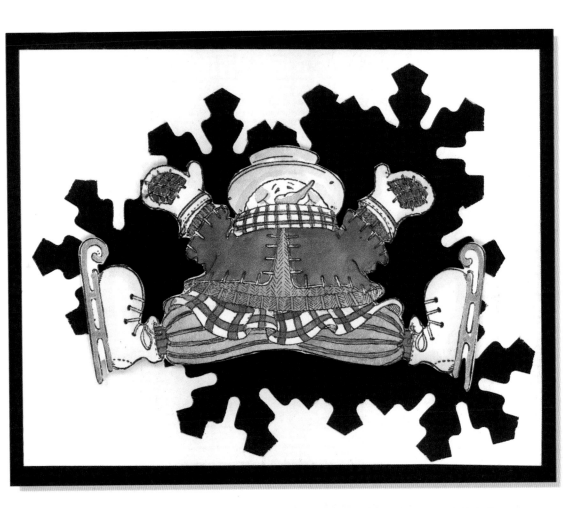

CREATING THE PROJECT

1. Create the frame by punching cardstock with a large snowflake punch in a random pattern leaving lots of room for the star. Mount on a dark card.

2. On a separate piece of white cardstock, stamp, watercolor, and silhou-ette the skater.

3. With a silver paint pen, highlight the ice skate runners.

4. Mount the skater in the center of the frame with foam mounting tape. Be sure to put enough tape to support the figure.

TIP

Balancing the proportions of images and frames creates a unified composition.

WINDOW TO IRELAND by Marcia Cooke

This approach to framing the focal point works just like a double-hung window. Tan cardstock offsets the green misty fields of the photo. The stamped shamrocks complement the photograph of the lush Irish countryside behind the panes—a great St. Patrick's Day card, or a wonderful way to present your travel photos.

CREATING THE PROJECT

1. Stamp the window in the center of the card and emboss the window frame.
2. Stamp, emboss, and color the shamrocks around the window.
3. Cut out the window panes using a craft knife.
4. Mount the photo behind the window.

SPRING VIOLETS

Spattering ink on a surface adds an interesting background texture without detracting from the main image.

CREATING THE PROJECT

1. Stamp the image on white cardstock with black archival ink.
2. Watercolor the flowers and leaves. Lightly spatter a background (an old toothbrush works beautifully).
3. Stencil or hand draw vertical background lines with watercolor pen and pull color with water on a brush.
4. Trim the image with deckle-edge scissors and mount on complementary paper.

FRAMED FLOWERS

Edge-trimmed flowers burst out of their frame in this colorful, three-dimensional design, suggesting the robust growth of a healthy garden. We have accentuated the flower burst by trimming around the petals that project outside the frame. The off-white mat behind the image lifts it off the page. The frame idea is further developed with the shape, size, and placement of the plum-colored mat.

CREATING THE PROJECT

1. Stamp the image on tan paper with black pigment ink and emboss using clear embossing powder.
2. Cut out along the outline and paint with pigment ink to allow sufficient time for blending the colors.
3. Layer on complementary colors to form a card.

FLOWER VASE GIFT CARD

Small images can easily get lost in a card design, but not when you accent them with a window frame and a nicely cut edge. In this lovely gift card, the bow is almost as big as the image, yet the frame teases the eye directly to the stamp.

CREATING THE PROJECT

1. Fold the card and punch or cut the window.
2. Glue liner paper to the inside of the card and stamp the image so it shows through the window. Color in the image with brush markers.
3. Cut the front of the card shorter than the back using a decorative edger.
4. Punch a hole for the ribbon and tie the bow.

ROSE CARD

A frame does not always have to encircle an image. Sometimes a frame that is implied is just as strong. Here the soft green border along the right edge extends the visual size of the card and makes as strong a statement as a four-sided containing frame. The silhouetted leaf breaks the form of the foreground extending the eye beyond the central focus. On this petite note card, the rose, leaves, and flower stem were outlined and detailed with embossing, then the rose was colored with blended watercolors. The silhouetted leaf is beautifully accented by the moss green paper.

CREATING THE PROJECT

1. Stamp the flower on white cardstock and emboss in gold. Make a mask of the flower and place it over the flower.
2. Stamp the leaves slightly overlapping the mask so that the leaves will appear behind the flower when the mask is removed.
3. Draw the flower stem by hand, extending it over the bottom edge of the card. Emboss the leaves and stem.
4. Watercolor the leaves and flower.
5. Trim the opening edge of the card shorter than the card back, silhouetting a portion of the leaf.
6. Glue a contrasting paper to the card back.
7. Edge the card back with a gold paint pen.

WATERLILIES AND DRAGONFLY

Cut shapes can mimic those from nature. Here diagonal zigzags that reiterate the waterlily petals quietly corner and frame the soft central image. The watery, soft colors called for a seamless transition to the spring green card. The dragonfly hovers above the waterlilies and is actually constructed of three punched dragonflies to add dimension. Details *are* important.

CREATING THE PROJECT

1. Stamp the waterlilies using black archival ink.
2. Punch out three dragonflies, one from vellum and two from cardstock. Cut the wings off the cardstock ones and the tail off the vellum one. Cut a piece of thin wire approximately three inches long.

3. Sandwich the vellum and wire between the two cardstock bodies. Bring the wire straight down at the end of the body and coil the wire.

4. Punch a 1/16-inch hole through the cardstock, insert the dragonfly's coiled wire, and attach at the back with a piece of tape.

5. Punch the slot zigzags in the corners of the background paper.

6. Insert the waterlilies cardstock as you would a picture, and mount on a card.

SENSATIONAL ARTICHOKE
by Joyce Hazen

Punched corners on the purple paper layer and a stippled "torn-paper" edge on the top layer add texture and visual weight to this busy collage of images. The torn paper effect is accomplished by masking the collage to allow stippling in the shape of a torn edge. The one-sided frame is all that is necessary since the two layered mats complete the picture. The dark, uneven edge refocuses our attention on the dominant image.

CREATING THE PROJECT

1. Ink the artichoke with brush markers and stamp on coated paper.

2. Cut a mask to cover the artichoke and stamp around it with various stamps inked with brush markers.

3. Remove the mask, apply ink to some of the words, and stamp them over all the other stamps.

4. Stipple the edge. To create the look of torn paper, use a torn piece of scrap paper as a mask. Lay the mask over the stampings, then tap a stipple brush repeatedly onto the card. Use the same colors for stippling as you used for stamping.

5. Punch out the corners of the frame with a corner punch and layer the card.

LETTER COLLAGE

A muted platform for an elegant central image makes a consistent statement of support. Our artist worked from the postage stamp art to select the palette for the background and frames. This is a wonderful example of training your eye to observe your surroundings and discover that ideas are everywhere. In this card, a compilation of many small shapes conveys a formal sense of refinement and elegance. A small deckle-edge gives the top paper layer of this card a formal look that's made vintage by inking with a gold leafing pen and the watermark ink at the bottom of the frame.

CREATING THE PROJECT

1. Collect materials to support the theme of the postage stamp—the main image here.
2. Stamp the words and reduce on a copier to better fit the size of the card. Copy onto parchment-colored paper and stamp the fleur-de-lis at the top with dusty plum pigment ink. Construct a tiny envelope of the same paper.
3. Trim the pink paper with the deckle-edge scissors, stamp the inkwell with peacock gold, and outline the paper with gold leafing pen.
4. Assemble the elements, and glue.
5. Highlight the scallop of the envelope with gold. Highlight the fleur-de-lis, inkwell, and ink. We used a dip pen and gold ink.
6. Leave a large border at the bottom of the second layer, and stamp with watermark ink.
7. Mount onto a third layer. Stamp corner images in gold ink.

TIP

To apply craft glue, squeeze the glue onto a piece of scrap paper and pick it up with a toothpick or wooden skewer to transfer to the ornaments or paper. A little goes a long way. This glue dries quickly and remains flexible—what you have attached will not pop off the card.

FALLEN LEAVES

A soft background can add richness and depth to a simple image. The background cardstock is first colored with a small ink pad/applicator and then blended to soften and mix the colors.

CREATING THE PROJECT

1. Stamp the leaves on tan background paper with a roller stamp.
2. Color the paper with cat's eye pads in autumn colors, starting with the darker colors and finishing with the lighter ones.
3. Apply gold ink to the dots. Edge the layer with a gold pen.
4. Stamp and emboss the bare tree on cream stock. Cut the edge of the paper with deckle-edge scissors.
5. Mount on the leaves and layer to form a card.

ANTS ON THE MOVE

Shaped layered papers and a stamped horde of roving ants frame the delectable goodies in the picnic basket with wit and style. A dominant central image framed against two layers of dark solid colors stands centerstage against a background of smaller images. The red frame around the card ties it all together.

CREATING THE PROJECT

1. Stamp the ants with a roller stamp, moving it diagonally over the card. Continue until the surface is covered with ants.
2. Stamp the picnic basket, paint it with watercolors, and cut it out. Mount on navy blue cardstock.
3. Punch one corner of a piece of red cardstock with a notched corner punch, insert the navy stock into the corner to determine the size of the red stock. Cut the paper to that dimension, then punch the other three corners.
4. Insert the navy stock and mount everything on the ant paper. Mount the assembly to the card.

A MOMENT IN TIME by Joyce Hazen

Stamping on glossy coated paper with brush markers produces the brightest colors. Stippling, a variation of sponging, is an excellent way to create a shadow of gradations of blended colors. Tapping tiny dots with a special stippling brush results in a background rich with dimension and texture. Variations in color intensity are accomplished by layering the stippled dots; start with an overall light layer and build up to your desired effect. On this card, the color fades toward the center, creating a hazy glow around the unusual central figure, which is presented to us amid a fanciful depiction of the passage of time.

CREATING THE PROJECT

1. Ink the stamps with brush markers and stamp on coated paper. Overlap images and stamp some off the edges of the paper. Color the images on the paper as desired with brush markers.

2. Ink a stippling brush with an ink pad, then tap it around the outside edges of the paper. Repeat the colors of the markers used for stamping the images.

3. Edge the card with a gold paint marker.

TIP

When stamping with brush markers apply extra pressure to insure all the ink transfers from the stamp to the paper.

HONEYBEE CARD by Kim Smith

The honeycomb background of this card was made by repeatedly stamping the hexagon-shaped tip of a stylus onto cardstock. A background's size, shape, and color should set the stage for the main idea. In this project the soft honeycomb background provides the perfect setting for the featured stamped bee. The dark frame around the bee lifts it off the muted honeycomb.

CREATING THE PROJECT

1. Create the background with the stylus tip. For the multicolored effect shown, ink first in a parchment color pigment pad, then tap the edges into amber and terra cotta pads.
2. Stamp the bee on a small piece of cardstock. Frame and mount on top of the honeycomb background.

PAISLEY PRINT

A print is a print is a print . . . and in this case, the image is framed with old-fashioned photo corners. The glittery gold enhances the iridescent pastel tones of the liquid watercolor and the sponged-on gold.

CREATING THE PROJECT

1. To create the background, apply various colors of iridescent liquid watercolors to paper. Apply one color at a time, using a paint spreader, to move the paint to create an overlapping wavy pattern. Follow the pattern with each color and when completed sponge gold over the entire paper.
2. Ink the image using sepia black pigment ink and stamp over the background. Emboss with clear embossing powder.
3. Cut out and mount onto brown background paper to frame. Add the gold photo corners.
4. Mount the framed print onto complementary cardstock.

TIP

Lay the cardstock so that the main image can bleed off all sides without damaging your work surface.

ASIAN FAN COLLAGE
by Gwen Berg

An all-over background of color and texture can add as much interest to a card as any of the elements placed upon it. In this case the antiqued paper provides a distinctive support for the ornamental fan. It's fun to work with the shiny paper used to create the background of this project. The combination of ink and water creates complex marble-like results.

CREATING THE PROJECT

1. To create the background, put various colors of metallic markers onto glossy black cardstock and spritz with water to move the marker ink around. You may even use a straw and blow at the ink to move it. Let air dry.
2. Spray with gold webbing spray, then brayer with a foam brayer using gold metallic ink. Edge with a gold leafing pen.
3. Stamp the text on cream cardstock, tear, edge with a dark marker, and attach to background paper.
4. Use the metallic markers to create the background paper for the fan. When dry, stamp the fan stamp over the top using black archival ink.
5. Stamp and emboss the figures on the black glossy cardstock.
6. Arrange the elements in a pleasing manner and glue in place.
7. Layer and mount on a card.

TIP

Layering papers with contrasting colors and textures adds interest to any project. You can use paper layers to form a frame around an image you want to feature, or simply as a background. The deeper the colors you choose, and the more varied the textures of papers, the more dramatic the resulting effect will be. Layering is an easy way to make even the simplest card look sophisticated.

EMBOSSED OVAL FRAME

After stamping and embossing, the center of this frame was cut out and placed over the photo of the little girl. The frame was then attached to a ribbon—for another take on the same idea, make a hanging photo gallery by attaching several framed photos to a long length of ribbon.

WATERMARKED BACKGROUND

This soft background suggests the butterfly's habitat without overpowering the card's focal point. The gauzy ribbon adds another dimension, mimicking a butterfly's fragile wings. Another way—not quite literal—of framing the butterfly.

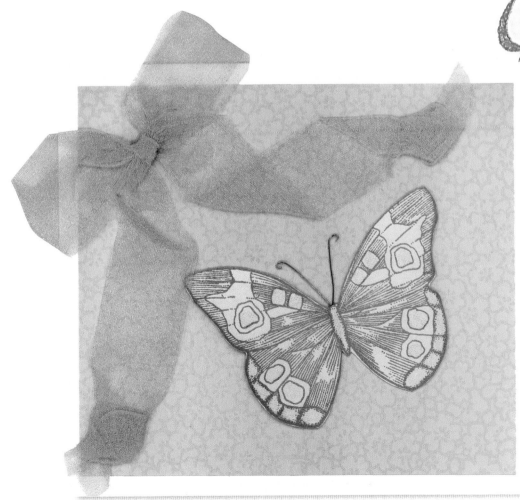

CREATING THE PROJECT

1. Ink the butterfly stamp with metallic gold, daub on various colors to highlight the butterfly, then stamp using exra pressure. Fill in any open areas with colored pencils.
2. Cut out the butterfly, bringing the wings forward, and attach a wire antennae.
3. Ink the background stamp with watermark ink and stamp.
4. Layer the card and attach the butterfly and ribbon.

EMBOSSING

mbossing works like magic to raise a stamped image off the page and to give it extraordinary luster and depth. Yet in its most basic form it's a wonderfully simple technique. The process requires only a stamp, pigment or embossing ink, embossing powder, and a heat tool. Stamp the image using embossing ink, sprinkle embossing powder onto the wet ink (tap off any excess powder), and then melt the powder with a heat gun. As with any other stamping technique you'll find plenty of variations on the basic theme, but all provide a wonderful way to add exciting dimension to a project. Most people will have no idea how you achieved such a polished effect.

As well as being beautiful, embossing offers some practical benefits to stamp artists. The act of heatsetting the embossing powder makes the ink underneath resistant to fading when exposed to light. It also makes water-soluble ink impervious to moisture. And aside from the embossing powders themselves and a heat gun, you need no other special materials or tools. In addition, embossing works well on all sorts of papers, as well as on plenty of non-paper surfaces. Pigment ink is usually recommended for embossing because of its slower drying time, which means you won't have to rush when sprinkling on the embossing powder.

Once you've become familiar with basic embossing, you'll probably want to try your hand at other tools and materials, perhaps experimenting with embossing pens or fluids or some of the different types of powders such as glitter powder or "detail" powder, which is formulated to pick up fine lines in the stamped image.

Embossing gives stamped images luster and depth, so they seem to lift off the page. The process uses special embossing inks and powders, which you heat-set with a hot-air gun. These techniques help you add a professional finish to your stamped projects.

VELLUM ROSES

Embossing is effective on many different papers, including vellum. The roses and leaves in this project were embossed on the front surface, but colored on the reverse side. The result is misty, dream-like color with great depth.

CREATING THE PROJECT

1. Stamp the trellis on cardstock, then stamp and emboss the flowers on medium-weight vellum.
2. Color the flowers and leaves on the reverse side of the vellum with markers, using the lightest colors first. Outline the image with darker colors applied directly over the lighter colors.
3. Trim the vellum narrower than the cardstock width so that you have a wide band of vellum over the cardstock with "margins" of the trellis visible on either side.
4. Wrap the vellum around the cardstock.
5. Shape the corners of the trellis with a punch or deckle scissors and mount on the card.

SMALL BOOK

This small booklet, suitable for notes or sketches, features gold embossed edges on the flowers, leaves, stems, and frame. Building up the central oval shape gave it depth. We stamped the whole image twice, then silhouetted one oval and mounted it atop the oval on the full stamped image. This careful layering produced a delicate and distinctive project. The booklet can be as many pages as you wish—ours has twelve pages.

CREATING THE PROJECT

1. Make the book from text-weight paper sandwiched between cardstock covers. Corrugated trim hides the staples that hold the book together.

2. On cardstock, stamp and emboss the image twice. Paint inside the oval on one image, and outside the oval on the other.

3. Cut out the painted oval and attach it to the corresponding oval on the other image with small pieces of mounting tape so it stands off the surface.

4. Layer onto decorative paper and fasten to the book.

5. String beads onto wire and attach to the spine. Twist the wire into curls at the ends.

BABY HANDS

The luminous hands on this lovely birth announcement were stamped with clear embossing ink, then sprinkled with opaque white embossing powder and heated. The soft color and texture of the paper and the deckled edge add style to this simple card. To avoid scorching, keep a careful eye on the artwork when heating the embossing material. Try a few practice sessions first to see how long to apply the heat.

CREATING THE PROJECT

1. Stamp and emboss one hand using clear embossing ink and opaque white embossing powder. Working on one hand at a time ensures the best coverage of embossing powder while the ink is still wet.

2. Stamp and emboss the second hand.

3. Punch two small holes on the fold of the card. If you fold the card and then punch using a circle with half the punch off the fold you will have the holes punched right on the fold.

4. Insert the ribbon into the holes and tie a pretty bow.

FRIENDSHIP CARD

The theme of a project can direct its composition and color. Here, the gold-embossed "Peace" strongly emphasizes the message while visually balancing the gold lock and key and strengthening the overall composition of the collage. The message of friendship and world peace suggested by the special postage stamp mounted just above center is calmly reiterated in the soft mauve tones as well as in the collage elements themselves.

CREATING THE PROJECT

1. Collect the items and stamps to support the theme of the collage. In this card, the postage stamp is the key image.
2. Emboss the "Peace" stamp.
3. Ink and stamp the other images, and add color to coordinate with the papers.
4. Assemble to please the eye.

ELEGANT BUTTERFLY

Embossing is an elegant way to bring to life the thin lines of detailed images. In this project, the "detail" gold embossing powder used on the butterfly is accented by the gold-stamping on the layer underneath it. The sumptuous dark burgundy cardstock needs little more color to complete its statement. The muted color pencil tones merely hint at deeper reserves, and the gold embossing adds a sophisticated finish.

CREATING THE PROJECT

1. Stamp and emboss the large butterfly on the burgundy cardstock.
2. Color the butterfly with colored pencils.
3. Stamp the swirl design on the first background paper (green) in gold. Stamp the design on the second background paper (burgundy) in black.
4. Glue the layers together, outlining the background layers with a gold paint pen. Layer to form a card.

SUBTLE KIMONO

Resist embossing is another interesting technique. It lets you preserve the color of the background paper to incorporate it into the design. When using embossing as a resist technique, stamp the part of the image you want to maintain the color of the paper with clear embossing ink, then emboss with clear embossing powder. After embossing, you can color the rest of the image—the embossed areas won't absorb any color, but you will need to wipe clean the area that was embossed to remove the excess ink. Here the kimono is layered on a background of Japanese letters; the gold cord down the card fold suggests a sash and provides a subtle finishing touch.

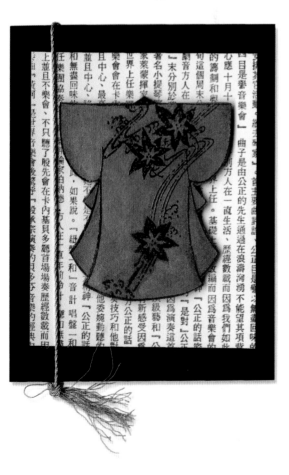

CREATING THE PROJECT

1. Stamp the kimono on black paper with clear embossing ink.
2. Sprinkle the outline and robe details with clear embossing powder, tap off the excess, and heat.
3. Color the kimono with metallic gold paint. With a dry tissue remove the paint from the embossed area before it dries.
4. Stamp the background image on lightweight cardstock.
5. Layer the stamped background onto a glossy black card and mount the kimono on top with foam mounting tape. Attach the gold cord.

..LET IT SNOW...LET IT SNOW...LET IT SNOW!

EMBOSSED SNOW

Textured embossing powders like that used for the snowflakes on this navy blue background don't add shine like other embossing powders, but you can mix different embossing powders (and there seem to more types on the market every day) to produce interesting effects. The right mix of embossing powders—half opaque white and half iridescent sparkle in this case—enhances our wintry design with shimmering snow. Apply the powder mixture just like regular embossing powder, then heat to raise the surface. This card also features fleece-topped mittens made from liquid appliqué and a twisted rope that's right in step with the season.

CREATING THE PROJECT

1. Make the rope by twisting or braiding white and red cord.
2. Punch out four mittens—two punched mittens per hand—and sandwich an end of the rope between each front and back.
3. Apply white liquid appliqué to the mitten tops—one side at a time—and heat to raise. Sprinkle with glitter.
4. Stamp and emboss a snowflake on each mitten, using the embossing mix described above with clear embossing ink.
5. Stamp the greeting.
6. Punch a small hole near the top of the card, insert a brad from which to hang the mittens, and tie a bow above the brad.
7. To create the snow frame, ink a sponge dauber with clear embossing ink and pat repeatedly on the card. Use the same mix for the background as for the snowflakes that adorn the mittens.

TILE CARD

Double-embossing creates both a raised surface and shiny, luminous color that suggests glazed ceramic tile to some, stained glass to others. It isn't difficult, it just adds a step. Start by stamping and embossing the image as usual. After coloring the image, emboss the entire surface with clear embossing fluid and clear powder to create the shiny, smooth topcoat. The result is brilliant: a raised surface that offers texture as well as luminous color. The project shown here uses a tile stamp, which simulates the look of a hand-painted ceramic tile.

CREATING THE PROJECT

1. Stamp and emboss the image in black ink on cardstock.
2. Color with brush markers.
3. Cover the entire image with clear embossing ink and emboss with clear embossing powder.
4. With a swirl punch, punch the swirls out of the four corners.
5. Mount the "tile" to the card.

GLITTER FISH by Elaine E. Elwick

Special effects powder produces exactly that—the opportunity to create special effects. The powder pops off the surface when heated, and turns sticky enough to grab brushfuls of pearlescent powders, gold leafing flakes, or whatever decorative materials you choose for adorning your designs. Lightly reheating the surface with a heat gun sets the decorations securely in the raised surface. Release your imagination and the end product will be as captivating as only a one-of-a-kind artwork can be.

TIP

A punch that has direction, or "handedness," like the small swirl that decorates the corners of the tile card, can be reversed simply by turning the paper over before punching.

CREATING THE PROJECT

1. Stamp and emboss the image with special effects embossing powder. Don't overheat, or the powder will lose its "stick."
2. While hot, brush on decorative materials, and heat again to set. Clean off excess with a cotton ball.
3. Stamp bubbles with tinted embossing ink and apply pearl powder with a dry brush. Clean off excess with a cotton ball.
4. Cut the image panel square and draw a border with a silver paint pen.
5. Cover cardstock with a sheet of double-stick adhesive. Peel off the liner to expose the sticky surface and mount the image panel.
6. Cover the rest of the card stock with pearl powder, beads, glitter, and gold-leaf flakes.
7. Spray the surface with acrylic spray to seal.

FLOWERS AND BUTTERFLIES by Frankie Fioretti

If you like the look of double-embossing, experiment with ultra-thick embossing powder. This powder can be used in a variety of ways to produce fresh, innovative designs. The process is the same as with regular embossing, but repeat the stamp-sprinkle-heat steps until you've built up layers to the thickness you want. You can leave the thick surface as is, or stamp into it, or even impress beads or other embellishments into it. If you want to develop an antiqued, stressed appearance, build up a lot of layers. The thickness will make the material prone to cracking, which will produce that time-worn effect you're after. If the material should crack and a crackled look wasn't part of your original plan, evaluate the project before you throw it into the trash. The new surface may surprise you by accentuating the design in an unanticipated but delightful way. Remember, sometimes the best results come from serendipity.

CREATING THE PROJECT

1. For the central image color the paper and stamp with the flower.

2. Apply embossing fluid and and ultra-thick embossing powder. Heat, and while still warm add more powder and then heat again. You can sprinkle a small amount of dry paint pigment into the hot embossing powder.

3. When you have built up a couple of layers of embossing, ink the flower with pigment ink and stamp while the embossing is still hot. This technique is best done on thick cardstock or thin shirtboard to support the thick embossing.

4. Mount the panel on silver foil paper, layered on lightweight mauve cardstock and then burgundy cardstock edged with silver.

5. Mount the completed panel slightly lower than center on background paper colored with a stylus color tool and stamped with butterflies.

GILDING THE LILY

This simple fleur-de-lis illustrates the mileage you can get from a single design by the artful application of embossing powders, adhesive, and glitter. In each case the artist has taken pains to harmonize the colors in the motif with the colors in the background and frame papers. It's fun to create a series like this one, using a bold stamp you enjoy, and it's a worthwhile challenge to expand the series as far as your time and materials will allow. You'll probably come up with a few combinations that just don't work, along with some surprising ones that do.

PUNCH ART

With only a handful of punches and a stack of paper, you can create projects that range from whimsical to stunning. All you need to add is some information and your imagination. That's why punch art is so wonderful and why many people are using punches when decorating cards or gifts and embellishing invitations or stationery.

Punch artists often create around themes that support a design or existing photos. For example, an artist working on a Mother's Day card might enhance it with punched flowers or baby animals, while an artist designing a Christmas card might scatter holly leaves along its border. One of the best things about punch art is that you don't need to have a flower punch to make those flowers or a leaf punch for your leaves. All things are made up of shapes. Put together in different ways, these shapes create forms—a tiny sunburst can be the center of a blooming flower. You can use punched shapes flat or folded, cut apart, or piled into bountiful 3-D images. This is when the real fun of punch art begins—when you begin playing with the basic punched shapes. Through your choice of solid and printed papers and the way you put together the shapes, you create a unique piece of art.

Remember to look carefully at the positive punched shape as well as the negative shape or space left in the cardstock when you punched the shape. Both images are usable—sometimes on the same project. Or you might want to save the positive punched shape for later use.

The possibilities of punch art are endless and waiting to be explored. So get out your punches, paper, and adhesives and step into the wonderful world of punch art.

Love is in the air

To create three-dimensional effects, try combining paper punches with rubber-stamped images. As you can see in the examples on this page, sometimes you'll want to keep the punched-out piece to use as a floating element above the basic card, while in other situations you'll use the punched-out hole as a window through the card.

BEARS TO BOYS

With a little creative thinking, you'll probably find that you can use a single punch in a variety of ways. These little charmers all come from the same large bear punch, but are trimmed and decorated in different ways. The punched bear can be dressed up or down, adorned with paper clothing or a punched bow, or even—minus ears—transformed into a baby or a gingerbread boy. With a little experimentation, the cards shown can be even further customized to work with different greetings.

We're tickled pink!

VARIATIONS ON A THEME: CREATING THE PROJECTS

SEWING-CARD BEAR

Punch the bear out of brown cardstock and dress with a punched-out bow. Add details with a pen. Mount on a background trimmed with a decorative paper edge. To color the edge, hold the background paper firmly against scrap paper and run a brown brush marker along the edge.

WE'RE TICKLED PINK!

Punch the bear out of brown cardstock, then dress it with plain or printed paper cutouts— punched out, of course!—and trimmed to fit the brown bear. Draw the details by hand.

GINGERBREAD BOY

Punch the bear out of cinnamon-colored stock. Trim off the ears and upturned parts of the feet. Add details with white and burgundy gel pens.

RAINBOW BEAR

Using a brayer and a pastel rainbow pad, color a piece of coated cardstock (right). Cut a piece of double-sided sheet adhesive slightly larger than the bear. Remove one side to expose the adhesive and lay it on the brayered cardstock. Punch out the bear. Expose the other side of the double-sided adhesive and apply clear glass (holeless) beads. Mount on background paper. Punch along the bottom edge with a film strip punch and string ribbon through. Mount on a card.

FOLDED BEAR GIFT CARD

Fold text-weight paper in half and insert the folded edge into the bear punch. Turn the punch over to make sure that the folded edge won't quite be cut when you punch. Punch two bears out of blue cardstock. Mount the blue bears on either side of the folded bears (the covers). Draw the details with a white gel pen.

LITTLE STAR

Punch the bear out of flesh-colored cardstock and trim off the ears. Punch another bear from white cardstock and cut to form a diaper. Draw the details by hand and mount on a star; use as a closure for a card or on an envelope.

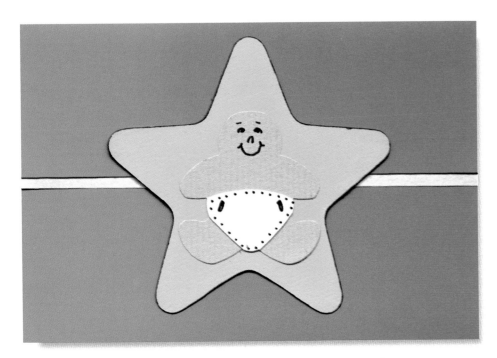

HEARTS AND PHOTO CARD

Many pictures have interesting areas, but on the whole may not be good enough to make it into the family photo album or scrapbook. Don't toss them out—instead, punch out the interesting parts and mount them on a card with other punched shapes.

CREATING THE PROJECT

1. Punch hearts out of three printed papers and a photo of someone special.
2. Mount in a square and layer onto a background that's been trimmed with a decorative edge. Frame the square with a darker color.
3. Mount on a card.

NATURE'S BEST

Dried leaves and flowers make wonderful greeting-card adornments that add interest and texture against simple backgrounds.

CREATING THE PROJECT

1. Purchase dried flowers or dry your own.
2. To frame the dried flower, punch out a circle from the top layer of cardstock and mount on a lighter color and then on a card.
3. Using tweezers to hold the dried flower and fern, apply glue to secure them within the punched area.

BIRTHDAY CANDLE

Even simple tools can be used to create sophisticated results. Here ordinary circle punches were used to form the shape at the heart of this birthday greeting.

TIP

The pointed tips of a self-closing tweezers make it easy to remove the liner from mounting adhesive.

CREATING THE PROJECT

1. Ink the stamp with marker and stamp on a card.
2. Punch the biggest circle out of cardstock and mount in the center of the stamping. Punch the smaller circle out of mounting adhesive, remove one of the liners, and place the adhesive in the center of the larger circle. Remove the other liner and apply glitter.
3. Punch the candle from white paper. Place the same piece of paper with the candle punched out into the smaller circle punch. It helps to turn the punch over so you can see the candle shape to make sure it's centered.
4. Cut two pieces of mounting tape, place on either side of the candle in the punched circle, and mount on top of the glitter.

PUNCHED STATIONERY

It's easy to personalize your writing paper with just a few punches. The scalloped squares are layered and the daisy applied; the gold center is cut with a circle punch.

CREATING THE PROJECT

1. Punch out three daisies and the largest squares out of dark blue paper.
2. Punch the small squares and the 1/8-inch circles out of gold paper.
3. For the banding, cut a narrow strip of dark blue and a narrower one of gold
4. Layer as shown on text-weight paper.

WE WISH YOU A MERRY CHRISTMAS
Punched silver stars accentuate this lovely card. They're so simple to create, but imagine this musical card without them!

CREATING THE PROJECT
1. Stamp the music on the front of cardstock.
2. Cut a piece of green cardstock one-half the size of the front of the card and mount it on the front of the stamped cardstock.
3. Punch out three silver stars and mount them over the seam with glue.

FLEUR-DE-LIS
Corner punches can be used to punch along a paper edge, not just in the corners. Just temporarily remove the punch corner guides to create lace.

CREATING THE PROJECT
1. Hold the punch with the corner guides removed so you can see the cutting edge. Punch the fleur-de-lis, beginning in the center to ensure that the cuts are symmetrically spaced out toward each side. Then continue punching on either side, making sure the edges overlap slightly.
2. Stamp the greeting and emboss.
3. Layer the punched and stamped stock over darker cardstock, so the lacy edge is highlighted.
4. Use a long-reach punch to make a pair of holes for the ribbon.

CARDS IN THE MAIL

Everybody loves interactive cards—there's something satisfying about relating to a card in a hands-on way. This card features a bright red heart that the recipient removes from the letterbox and opens to reveal the message.

CREATING THE PROJECT

1. Stamp the mail slot in the center of the front of the card. Using a craft knife, cut out the slot. Mount a piece of paper on the inside of the card, leaving 1 inch below the mail slot free of glue.
2. Fold a piece of red cardstock in half and place into a heart punch so that the fold is near the top and will not be cut when you punch out the shape.
3. Stamp or write a message on the inside of the heart and insert into the mailbox slot.

STARS AND GLITTER

This project uses punches to create masks and two-sided adhesive sheets to grab the colorful glitter.

CREATING THE PROJECT

1. Cut a 3 1/2-inch square and a 4-inch square from two-sided adhesive. Remove one of the liners from the smaller square and mount the adhesive onto a piece of text-weight paper. Trim the paper to the same size as the adhesive.
2. Remove the other liner and punch out stars (two sizes) and swirls from the liner to form masks. With a tweezers, firmly mount the stars and swirls glossy side down on the adhesive. Place some of them partially off the square.
3. Pour on the silver background glitter, pressing it down firmly to make sure it sticks to the adhesive.
4. Remove the swirl masks and add the gold glitter.
5. Remove the star masks one at a time and add the blue and red glitter.
6. Remove the liner from the 4-inch square of adhesive and mount it onto the card. Remove the other side and center the glittery square on top. Shake on blue glitter to form the border.

HOP TO THE LILY PAD

When you're deciding whether to use the positive cutouts (the shaped bits of paper) or the negative spaces (the holes cut in the paper) in your design, take a moment to consider using both. Combining both the cutouts and the punched holes in a single design not only lets you take full advantage of your punching tools, it can help you introduce pleasing repetitious rhythms, create depth, and impart a trick-the-eye feeling of motion when the positive cutout seems to be jumping out of the punched space. Here, the paper frog leaps above his underwater friends on a successful journey to the lily pad.

CREATING THE PROJECT

1. Punch three frogs near the bottom of pink cardstock, varying their positions. Punch two additional frogs out of green cardstock. You will be using the three frog-shaped holes in the pink and two green frog shapes.
2. Stamp and color the lily pads onto the pink cardstock sheet.
3. Glue together the two green frogs, sandwiching a 2-inch piece of 26-gauge wire between them. Wind two coils in the wire close to the frog with a thin knitting needle or wooden skewer.
4. Punch a tiny hole near one lily pad. Insert the end of the wire and tape to the back of the paper.
5. Mount onto green corrugated stock to add textural interest to the three frog shapes.
6. Layer to form a card.

STRING OF FLOWERS by Lara Zazzi

It's possible to layer punched cutouts the same way you would flat papers. Like flat papers, layered cutouts build up dimension in a project. The cutouts can be glued to the paper or secured any way you can dream up. Try more imaginative treatments, such as stringing them on elastic cord as shown. Here the black cord matches the base cutouts, unifying the design; in addition, the cord's starkness is a pleasant contrast to the rounded form of the flowers.

CREATING THE PROJECT

1. Punch out three large flowers and three smaller ones from two complementary colors of cardstock.
2. Stack the cutouts as shown on the facing page, then cut 1/4-inch slits through both layers.
3. String the flowers onto elastic cord. Punch two holes in the card and string the cord through, taping the ends on the inside of the card.
4. Cut a piece of cardstock the same size as the front of your card and glue to the inside to conceal the taped string edges.
5. Stamp the greeting.

DRAGONFLIES

Corner punching is especially effective on layered papers, where you can repeat the pattern on all the layers of the card. In this project, the scalloped corners of the paper echo the motion of the featured punched dragonfly as well as the images on the background layer.

CREATING THE PROJECT

1. Stamp the circle design on cream cardstock and cut it out.
2. On contrasting paper, punch out two large dragonflies.
3. Stamp the small dragonfly randomly around the edge of the background layer.
4. Corner-punch both paper layers.
5. Glue the layers together and attach the stamped silhouetted circle.

PINK POSIES by Gwen Berg

Punched shapes can be heaped or sculpted into bountiful 3-D images. For an eye-catching bouquet, glue an arrangement of punched shapes together to form small flowers, adorning each with a tiny center made with a punch. If you're working with larger flowers, you can give them various shapes after punching by rolling them around a wooden skewer. To create realistic-looking rounded flowers, petals can be pressed into a depression created in pliable carving material. Make leaves with a leaf punch or circle punch. Either vein them lightly with a stylus or fold them lightly in the center to shape them to complement your particular bouquet. Using these techniques, you can create magnificent floral arrangements with a fairly simple palette of colors and practically no adornment beyond a vase or other container. The sculpted images speak for themselves in a language of elegance and sophistication.

This captivating project uses seven punches, but the results are well worth it. The bouquet is arranged within a stamped and watercolored flowerpot and adorned with a lively punched frog.

CREATING THE PROJECT

1. Ink the flowerpot stamp with a dark green brush marker and stamp on watercolor paper. With a wet paintbrush, pull the outline color to the center of the pot. Silhouette the flowerpot and glue onto cardstock, which has been cut with decorative scissors and stippled using light purple ink.

2. Punch out the pink flowers using a giant flower punch. Cut between each petal toward but not touching the center of the flower. To shape each flower, push it down into carving material with the dull side of a pen or pencil.

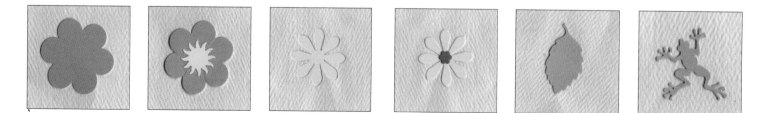

3. Punch out a yellow center with a sun punch and shape it in the carving material. Glue a center to each flower punched from a corner lacing punch.

4. Make the yellow flowers with a daisy punch.

5. To make a bud, roll one or more of the pink flower petals of the giant flower around a skewer, then glue it to hold the shape.

6. Punch the leaves and vein them with a bone folder or stylus. Bend slightly along the center line to shape.

7. Arrange the flowers and leaves, gluing in place with a strong glue that dries quickly and stays flexible.

8. Mount the decoratively edged card onto gold cardstock.

9. Punch out the jaunty frog and glue at the foot of the flowerpot.

TIP

Small sun punches make great flower centers; curl them by pressing into the pliable carving material.

A BASKET OF HYDRANGEAS by Gwen Berg

In this sophisticated basket of flowers the subtle color of the peach hydrangeas comes from sponging colors on the paper before punching. We adapted a flower corner punch to make our hydrangeas.

CREATING THE PROJECT

1. Stamp the basket on paper and cut it out (we used dark brown ink on tan paper). Give the basket shape by curling it over a round object such as a drinking glass before attaching it to the cardstock.

2. Place a small piece of mounting tape at the top center of the basket, to help it hold its shape, and glue the sides and bottom of the basket to cardstock.

3. Punch out circles of various sizes from paper suede for the leaves, then trim them with deckle scissors. Vein the leaves with an embossing tool.

4. Sponge cardstock to the desired color and punch out with a corner punch to get two different sizes of flowers.

5. Punch out flower centers from contrasting paper with 1/8- and 1/16-inch punches and glue them to the flowers.

6. To assemble, hold each flower with a self-closing tweezers, apply glue with a wooden skewer, and glue the flowers to the card. Make a base for the rounded puffs of flowers by punching out a short tower of circles in the same paper as the flowers and gluing them to shape. Then attach the flowers around and on top of the base.

7. Add the leaves and cut strips of paper for the stems.

8. Mount on a card and embellish with ribbon.

SPECIAL EFFECTS

An arsenal of materials stands ready to help you add special effects to your artwork. Throughout the book we have used all kinds of special effects—here we focus on several of them.

Some of the most eye-catching results come from dimensional products. Liquid appliqué, for example, puffs up when warmed with a heat gun. Dimensional adhesive, another fun medium, adds luster and gleam to stamped images, and rainbow-hued glitter creates a dazzling surface. Crackle finish is especially appealing if you're after an aged character suggestive of old cracked pottery pieces or tiles. Gold leaf is the ultimate special-effects material—by its very nature it suggests distinctive richness and preciousness.

While some special effects are typically built in (meaning that the surface is created from the inspired use of materials), embellishments are artfully arranged upon the surface of the paper to add depth and dimension. A quick visit to your local craft or stamp-supply store will reveal many inspiring materials for the buying, but there's no limit to what constitutes an embellishment—sewing baskets are treasure troves of rickrack, buttons, and trim materials, and flea markets offer all sorts of tempting baubles. Don't overlook nature's bounty in your search for special adornments. A glance around a field or yard on a crisp autumn day will reveal seeds, pods, dried grasses, and lots of other interesting materials just waiting to be harvested. Dried flowers are particularly versatile, as they come in many shapes and colors.

You can use many common stamping techniques to produce embellishments for your projects. Punching is a versatile technique, and the cutouts make great adornments, especially when punched from special papers. Another technique that provides infinite embellishment options is layering, using either commercially purchased or individually stamped papers.

From simple to complex, anything's possible once you break free from the surface of the stamped page. The flower far left is made by repeating a simple oval shape; the ladybug charm brings it to life. The butterfly (top right) lifts off the page, while the stained glass effect (lower right) comes from coloring the back of acetate.

*P*rojects that pop, pull, or take up space in three dimensions are definite attention grabbers, but they're just at the tip of the iceberg. More subtle 3-D touches speak with a softer voice, but can make just as big a statement. Whether you go for the showy or the understated, 3-D projects are as fun to make as they are to receive. Go where your sense of design leads you. On a larger scale, interactive pull- and pop-motion projects create fun and surprising effects. These types of 3-D devices involve card recipients physically as well as emotionally and send a message in a way that is sure to be remembered.

Small pieces of paper folded into interesting shapes are appealing and can be used in a variety of ways. Even something as simple as an attached folded envelope can underscore a message and add a memorable touch.

BEADED AND BEDAZZLING

Beads work well in a border or as an independent montage to dress up many types of cards. Here they're used to complement a postage-stamp collage.

CREATING THE PROJECT

1. Mount the stamp onto cardstock.
2. Cut apart a second identical stamp, mount on foam pieces, and place over the first stamp.
3. Cover parts to be highlighted with dimensional adhesive.
4. Create the background by drawing and tapping various ink pads onto a textured mat board. Mount the stamp image layer on the background.
5. Apply special bead adhesive in the area that will be decorated.
6. Add the beads and allow to dry.

GLISTENING MITTEN by Lara Zazzi

This project features a mitten glistening with fine snow. The snow is made from ultra-fine glitter cut to prism shapes so they'll reflect back ambient colors.

merry christmas

CREATING THE PROJECT
1. Use a bock stamp for the background.
2. Stamp the mitten and snowflake design.
3. Brush adhesive onto the mitten and sprinkle on the glitter.
4. Stamp the greeting.
5. Layer to form a card.

═══════

═══════ TIP ═══════

Fine glitter may cling to parts of the card where you don't want it. To remove the excess glitter hold the card over a piece of blank paper and with your fingers apply a sharp "flick" to the back of the card.

FISH WINDOW by Frankie Fioretti
In this interesting project, the triptych format adds to the feeling that the material has been salvaged in pieces from an ancient ruin, even though it features contemporary images. Bottled crackle medium gives the project this time-worn look. The fish and shells are stamped over a triple block stamp—stamp once and get three rectangles.

═══════

CREATING THE PROJECT
1. Stamp and emboss the shells in the background.
2. Stamp the triple block stamp in the foreground. Mask off the windows and color the background with an inked sponge.
3. Mask off the background and between the windows, and stamp the fish and shells inside. Color the images and the water.
4. Emboss the edge using an embossing pen and gold embossing powder.
5. Assemble the card and apply two-part crackle medium following the directions on the bottle.

═══════

BUNNIES IN A ROW

The weaving pattern shown here suggests a basket. By repeating the colors of the bunnies' neck bows, the ribbons also help unify the design. The fluffy, glittery bunny tails rise above the surface, adding a little more texture and a lot more fun.

CREATING THE PROJECT

1. Stamp the bunnies with ink that becomes permanent. Use a stamp positioner if you want faultless alignment.
2. Watercolor the shadows and color in the bows.
3. Cut ten evenly spaced 1-inch slits across the bottom of the card. Weave the ribbons through the slits.
4. Layer the bunnies on printed paper and mount to the card.
5. Sparingly apply liquid appliqué to texture their tails, and sprinkle with glitter once you've applied heat.
6. Attach ribbons at the top of the card and tie a bow.

SOUTHWEST CARD

Liquid appliqué comes in a variety of colors. This card features a surface simulating an old animal skin that is made with brown liquid appliqué. Easy to create, the effect is interesting and unusual.

CREATING THE PROJECT

1. Tear the edge of a piece of cardstock. Squirt brown liquid appliqué onto a piece of aluminum foil and pick it up with a brayer. Once the brayer is cov-

ered, roll the liquid appliqué on the card-stock. Heat the paper with a heat gun from underneath until you get a leathered look.

2. Stamp the sun in the background and emboss in copper.

3. Stamp the petroglyph on the leather.

4. Trim the background with a deckle edger and highlight with a copper paint pen.

5. Attach turtle charms. Mount on a card.

THREE PEARS

You can use gold leaf in a variety of ways in rubber-stamped artwork. It can be applied straight, to create a multi-colored image, or even set behind a screen of window plastic to add deep gloss to the warm luster of the gold. Gold leafing comes in full 5 1/2-inch leaves and as flakes. Both the leaves and flakes are available in various colors. Leafing can be applied to glue that has become tacky or to sheets of adhesive. You can stamp using glue as an ink, and once tacky apply the leafing. Once the leafing covers the adhesive, brush the excess off with a dry, firm, flat stenciling-type brush. Save the excess flakes for future application.

CREATING THE PROJECT

1. Using foam sponge, apply leafing adhesive to the stamp. (It will become clear and turn tacky when dry.)

2. Immediately stamp on paper (the adhesive turns clear) and wash the stamp to remove any remaining glue.

3. When the adhesive is tacky add gold leafing flakes and adhere them by tapping gently. Remove excess leaf with a dry, flat-edged stencil-type brush.

AMY'S MAGIC by Amy Harpool

Clear window plastic (acetate) makes everything gleam. As shown in this project, it partners perfectly with glitter. When you sandwich glitter between cardstock and the plastic, it shines through with a magical glow.

CREATING THE PROJECT

1. Stamp on clear window plastic (acetate) with permanent ink. (Or stamp on paper and copy on the acetate.) When dry take a piece of double-stick adhesive remove one liner and apply the adhesive onto the image you have stamped on the window plastic. You will apply it to the same side as you stamped.
2. Trim the window plastic with the adhesive attached down to the frame. On the liner you removed, stamp again.
3. Blot to dry and cut out the images. Remove the remaining liner from the adhesive.
4. Mask the images.
5. Apply leafing or glitter to the background.
6. Using a pointed tweezers, remove the masks one at a time and apply various colors of glitter.
7. Mount on the card.

TIP

When stamping on shiny acetate it may be difficult to get a crisp dark print. Stamping on a piece of white paper and copying onto the acetate often provides a better result.

STAMPING WITH PLANTS

Some of the freshest stamps may be growing right outside your back door. This glorious card was made by inking real flower heads and leaves and using them as stamps.

CREATING THE PROJECT

1. Cut the stem off as close as possible to the flower.
2. Firmly push the flower down onto an ink pad with a piece of wax paper. Once it's well inked, press the flower onto the paper with a piece of tissue paper. You will need to ink the flower each time you stamp.
3. Repeat the process as desired, masking off the flower when you want to add leaves, ferns, or other background images.
4. Frame by mounting on contrasting paper and then attach to cardstock.

DRIED FLOWER EMBELLISHMENTS

This delicate dried blossom takes centerstage in this pretty, simple card.

CREATING THE PROJECT

1. Dry your flowers, ferns, leaves, etc., or purchase them.
2. Stamp the leaves on cardstock, and using a tweezers to hold the dried flower apply glue and place the flower in the center.
3. Mount on the card.

FLOWERY FOCAL POINT

Dried flowers make wonderful embellishments for greeting cards. This flower was framed with a fresh green frame stamp. Send one to a gardening friend and you'll be sure to harvest a big smile!

CREATING THE PROJECT

1. Purchase or dry your flowers. (Check out microwave devices to make drying your own flowers quick and easy.)
2. Stamp the frame on the cardstock and glue on the flower, holding it with tweezers for positioning.
3. Layer to form a card.

FLORAL ARRANGEMENTS

By combining simple shapes in interesting ways you can create a stunning card. Here, block stamps turned cornerways make a nice background for the deep-red dried flowers.

CREATING THE PROJECT

1. Dry your flowers, ferns, leaves, etc., or purchase them.
2. Using platinum metallic ink stamp the blocks twice with their corners touching.
3. Using a tweezers to hold the dried flower apply glue and mount the flower in the center over the blocks.
4. Mount on the card.

FLOWERY STATEMENTS
Stamped and dried flowers together make a cheery greeting for any occasion.

CREATING THE PROJECT
1. Dry your flowers, ferns, leaves, etc. They can also be purchased dried, or dried using flower presses, etc.
2. Stamp the flowers on cardstock, and silhouette.
3. Attach the dried leaves and silhouetted flowers to cardstock.
4. Mount on the card.

FRAMED DAISY by Kathy Perkins
If you look closely, you'll probably discover a host of inspiring "found" embellishments close at hand. These are the items that served a different purpose the first time around, and they're sure to add character and uniqueness to your artwork. Creativity can be fueled by just about anything, from the beads off a child's broken barrette to the old 35mm slide carrier featured here.

CREATING THE PROJECT
1. Stamp the daisy on a piece of white cardstock. Color in the flower's center.
2. Cover with a piece of vellum and mount behind the slide frame.
3. Mount on silver cardstock and then onto the card.

EMBOSSED EGYPTIAN COLLAGE by Kim Smith

Instead of using embossing powders and inks to build up a raised surface, the type of embossing used in this project raises the actual surface of the paper by pushing it against a metal stencil. For best results, use a light box when working with the metal stencil.

=== TIP ===

Rubbing some wax paper across the back of the project paper before beginning to emboss makes moving the stylus easier.

CREATING THE PROJECT

1. Place the stencil on the light box and cover with your paper. Run a stylus along all the open edges of the stencil to push them down.

2. Remove the stencil, place it on the front of the paper, and highlight the embossed designs with a dauber and dry paint pigment.

3. Lightly rub dry paint pigment powder over the background for shimmer.

4. Stamp the images on separate pieces of paper in brown ink. Tear around the edges and rub the surface and edges with pearl powders.

5. Arrange the elements and mount on a card.

BOUNTIFUL BIRTHDAY CAKES

Some stamps are available in both positive and negative images. The positive stamp produces a solid-colored image, the negative stamp creates a colored background leaving the featured image reversed out of the color. You can use these stamps in many ways, but this quilt background is one of the most effective. Watermark ink gives a rich tone-on-tone appearance that complements the background images.

CREATING THE PROJECT

1. Ink the positive and negative stamps with watermark ink and alternate stamping them on the card in quilt fashion.
2. Stamp the negative image on a small piece of cardstock to make a gift tag and stamp the message below.
3. Frame the gift tag and attach to the card with an eyelet.

DRAGONFLY'S GARDEN

In this card a dragonfly charm flits toward the stamped flower border, its image cleverly reproduced on the peach ribbon. Rich black ink graphically outlines the subtle tones of the colored pencils used to decorate this lovely thank-you card.

CREATING THE PROJECT

1. Stamp the flowers with black ink along the bottom edge of the cardstock.
2. Score and fold the card so the top edge stops at the flower border. Cut printed paper to wrap the card. On the back side, cut off the last inch and turn the paper to show the print along the front right edge. Glue in place.
3. Stamp the greeting on the inside.
4. Color in the flowers with pencils to match the paper and your ribbon.
5. Stamp the ribbon with gold ink and glue it, and the dragonfly charm, to the face of the card.

EMBELLISHED KIMONO

by Frankie Fioretti
This project features embell-ishments that work together to create an Asian motif.

CREATING THE PROJECT

1. On patterned resist paper, stamp the kimono with black archival ink. Paint the stamped image with copper metallic ink. Cut out the kimono and emboss the edge.
2. Wrap the kimono with various fibers.
3. Using resist paper with a different pattern, paint strips of complementary colors with a foam brush.
4. On the black layer, emboss leaves in copper.
5. Emboss the next layer using a sponge and embossing fluid with various colors of emboss-ing powder. Emboss the edge with copper.
6. Sponge the cardstock itself—the final layer of the card—with various iridescent and metallic inks.
7. Layer the papers on the cardstock and attach the wrapped kimono with foam mounting tape so it floats above the card.
8. To make the beads, cut long strips of paper the width of each bead, spread glue on the strips, and roll them around a toothpick or wooden skewer. When dry, paint with irides-cent and metallic paints and mount on a piece of painted skewer. Adorn with comple-mentary fibers.

POPPING BEARS

Pop-motion mechanisms, which cause images to spring to life the moment the card is opened, need be nothing more complex than an accordion-folded strip of paper attached to both flaps of the card, or a paper folded inward so that it erupts outward when the card is opened. These bears are stamped, cut out, folded, and attached at the ends—when the card is opened, they pop forward to greet the recipient. This card goes a step further by incorporating a sophisticated ribbon tie that matches the bows on the bears.

CREATING THE PROJECT

1. Stamp the bears in a row with their feet touching. Use a stamp positioner to line them up. Color, cut out, and score between the bears. Fold in the center so the bears are back to back. Fold the two end bears forward accordion-style. Attach the bow ties.
2. Cut the cover to 8 1/2 x 2 3/4-inches and the printed paper to 8 x 2 1/4-inches. Score and fold the cover twice—one side to measure 3 3/4-inches and the other side to measure 1 inch.
3. With a rectangle or squiggle punch, make a hole in the center of the 1-inch section and 1 1/4-inch in from the outside edge of the 3 3/4-inch section.
4. From the outside, string an 18-inch piece of narrow ribbon in one hole and out the other. Glue in the background paper to the inside of the card and over the ribbon.
5. Attach one bear to the edge of the 3 3/4-inch section. With the bears folded up, put glue on the back of the top bear and close the card.
6. String a bead onto each ribbon end and tie a knot.
7. To close the card, tie the ribbon in a bow.

DAD ON THE GO

Incorporating a sliding mechanism into a project makes it charmingly interactive and adds elements of fun and surprise. This card features a jazzy driver and some light-hearted dancing daisies that echo the motion of the card. A touch of clear glitter glue makes the car's lights gleam.

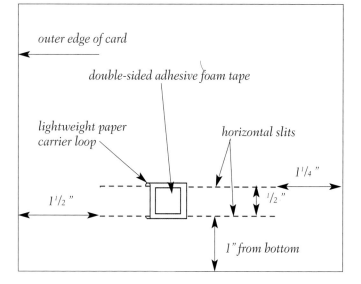

outer edge of card

double-sided adhesive foam tape

lightweight paper carrier loop

horizontal slits

1 1/4 "

1 1/2 "

1/2 "

1" from bottom

CREATING THE PROJECT

1. Stamp the greeting at the top of the card.
2. Stamp the flowers around the edges of the cardstock and color them with markers.
3. Cut and assemble the sliding mechanism as shown in the drawing.
4. Stamp the car and driver on scraps of colored paper, embellish as desired, and cut out. Tape the driver to the car.
5. Attach the pull tab to the car.
6. Attach the car and driver to the sliding mechanism.

Variation on a Theme— Valentine Driver

The "Dad-On-the-Go" project also works well without the sliding mechanism. Stamp the background card and the car-and-driver the same way, but float the assembled image on small pieces of foam tape to lift the central image off the background and give the car the illusion of movement.

A Potted Message

Shaped cards are always appealing, and if you can create the room to tuck in a little message, as this card does, so much the better. The flower stamp on the message turns the folded container into a flowerpot, but it could just as easily be manipulated to form a child's soldier hat or a small water cup.

CREATING THE PROJECT

1. Make an origami cup from text-weight metallic paper.
2. Mount onto a card.
3. On a piece of white cardstock, stamp the bouquet using archival ink. Paint with pearlescent paints. With a fine brush, edge the card with green ink.
4. Mount on a small card to create the insert to carry your secret message.

SIMPLE STAR

You can incorporate all sizes and shapes of folded papers into unique and memorable designs. This paper was colored and stamped first, then cut into teabag size and folded to create a star.

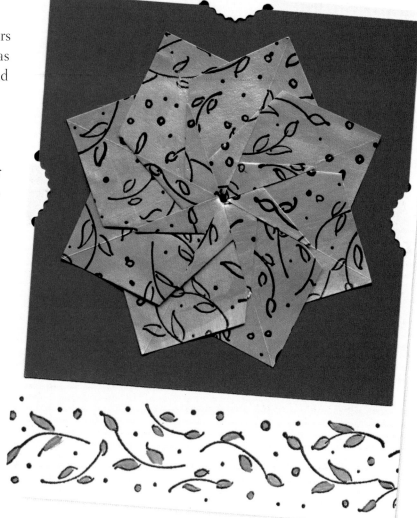

CREATING THE PROJECT

1. Color text-weight paper with paint, drawing it over the paper in small amounts with a paint spreader. Overlap colors as desired.

2. When the paper is dry, stamp the surface with a roller stamp.

3. Cut out eight teabag-size papers (2 in. x 2 in.) and fold them as shown in the drawing. Assemble to form the star.

4. Mount the assembled star on cardstock and layer to form a card. Use the same roller stamp to decorate the bottom of the card. Paint the open areas with the same paint you used on the teabag papers.

You will need 8 squares of paper.

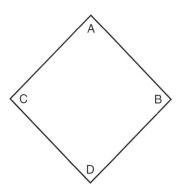

1. Begin with the wrong side of the paper facing up and the paper turned so the points are at the top, bottom, and sides.

2. Fold the paper in half vertically, wrong sides together, and bring point C to B. Open back up.

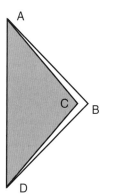

3. Fold the lower sides edges to the center fold line.

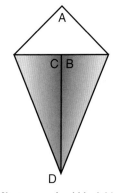

4. Your paper should look like the above diagram.

VELLUM STAR

Here's the basic shape made by folding eight squares of paper, as shown below. Folded vellum reveals the interior shapes, making the star look a lot more complicated than it actually is.

LOVE KNOT

Paper folding goes on and on as you try new folds. This love knot is just one more example.

5. Turn your paper over and fold point D up so it is even with the side points.

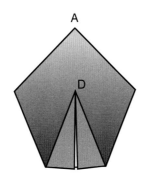

6. Your paper should look like the above diagram.

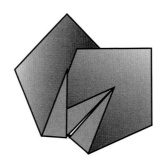

7. Place glue on lower right triangular side of first unit. Slide lower left side of second unit inside the pocket formed by the fold made in step 6, until it stops.

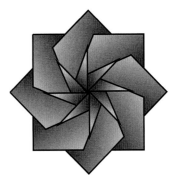

8. Continue in this manner, adhering eight units together being sure to finish by sliding the lower left corner of the first unit inside the pocket of the eighth unit.

LADYBUG, LADYBUG…

All the elements of this softly textured flower are made using a stylus instead of shaped or decorative stamps. The leaves on the stem and the petals, which are arranged in a pleasingly geometric pattern, are achieved by stamping the inked stylus, while the stem and grass are drawn with the same tool. You can stamp with any number of tools, or found objects. Test them out first, though, to make sure they will ink properly and won't leave any debris on the stamped surface.

CREATING THE PROJECT

1. Apply ink to the stylus tip and stamp petals to form a flower and leaves.
2. Use the tip's edge to draw the stem, grass, and leaf veins.
3. Blend ink at the bottom for grass.
4. Layer to frame and mount on a card.
5. Attach a ladybug charm.

SWINGING JACK

Capture the spirit of Halloween with this jaunty Jack-o-lantern. Mounted on layers of corrugated paper with wiggly wires, he pops off the card and out from a pile of brilliant autumn leaves.

CREATING THE PROJECT

1. Stamp the image and color.
2. Silhouette, cutting the pumpkins apart.
3. Crimp the two background papers and mount on the black card. Punch out two yellow and two black stars and several leaves out of scrap. Mount the yellow stars on Jack's hat, and the black stars and leaves on the crimped background.
4. Cut two 2-inch pieces of 24-gauge wire. Coil on a thin knitting needle or a wooden skewer and attach to the pumpkins with tape.

5. Attach the center pumpkin to the background with a coil of wire so it rises above the background about 3/4 inch.

FRIENDLY WITCH

This witch's curly coif comes courtesy of various colors of wire coiled around a thin knitting needle. She's a fun way to send somebody Halloween greetings.

CREATING THE PROJECT

1. Stamp the image twice. Color and cut one out. On the second image, cut out only the star and spider.
2. Mount the colored image on purple cardstock and cut freehand around the witch to form a frame.
3. Coil wire around a thin knitting needle. Punch one end of each piece through the edge of the hat and tape to the back.
4. Mount on black cardstock and trim freehand.
5. With a piece of foam mounting tape, mount the spider and star on the card.
6. Apply dimensional adhesive to the witch's face and the body of the spider.
7. Glue fine black beads to highlight the hat.

131

WOODLAND FLOWER

Stamping on wood is the same as stamping on paper, provided that you use the right type of ink. The combination of wood and stamped images is surprising by itself, but when you attach a piece of wood veneer to cardstock, as shown here, simple is elevated to stunning. When working with wood, use the grain to your advantage. Here the vertical flower stem and almost vertical leaves are enhanced by the vertical grain of the wood. When you're finished, spray the wood lightly with sealer to protect the image.

CREATING THE PROJECT

1. Stamp the wood veneer using craft ink.
2. When the ink is dry, spray lightly with sealer to protect the image.
3. Mount the veneer on cardstock.

TILE BOX by Jane Roulston

Putting lots of different shapes together can add interest to the simplest of objects. Here, squares, swirls, curls, and sunbursts combine to make this pretty little box.

CREATING THE PROJECT

1. Cut a piece of white shrink plastic about 90 percent larger than the desired size. Heat this test piece to determine the exact percent of shrinkage. Once determined, cut a new piece and sand in a crosshatch pattern with 320 or 400 grit sandpaper.

2. Stamp using crafters ink and cut apart.
3. Place on medium-weight cardboard in a regular or toaster oven set at 300 to 350 degrees Fahrenheit for approximately three minutes. You can also heat one piece at a time using a heat gun. After heating, the edges can be sanded if necessary.
4. Glue in place on top of a painted papier-mâché box for a tile effect.
5. Stamp and emboss the sides of the box using one of the images used on the shrink plastic.

LIGHT BOX by Kim Smith

Medium-weight vellum is easy to shape into a box with the help of a template. To hold the box together, use a transparent mounting adhesive—you don't want glue blotches to mar the vellum's sheerness. The swirls on this box were stamped on the surface, but the butterfly was colored from the reverse side of the vellum in rich jewel tones.

CREATING THE PROJECT

1. Trace the template on 28-lb. vellum and cut out along the lines. Stamp the design on the vellum, alternating colors. Blot off excess ink on clean paper.

2. Lightly score where indicated on the template with a bone folder.

3. Glue the vellum with two-sided adhesive. Cut it to the same size as the tabs, remove one liner, and apply it to the tab. Remove the other liner and attach to the box side.

4. Stamp the butterfly, blot, and color in the open areas from below, blotting between colors.

5. Cut out the butterfly and attach wire antennae.

6. Lightly score on either side of the body to raise the wings. Glue the body to the box.

TIP

Vellum will naturally curl if you press it lightly over a round object, such as a drinking glass. This property makes vellum ideal for representations of natural subjects, such as leaves, insects, and animals.

ILLUSTRATED GLOSSARY

SOURCES

ILLUSTRATED GLOSSARY

3-D STAMPING
3-D stamping is the process of attaching a cutout stamped image to an artwork with foam mounting tape or dots to raise it above the surface.
(*See page 45, top*)

DECORATIVE PAPER EDGERS
These are scissors especially designed to cut a decorative edge. are available in many shapes and sizes.
(*See page 49*)

BLOCK STAMPING
Block stamping is the technique of creating a background with a solid stamp, then stamping over it with a different image, usually in a different color. (*See page 40, top*)

DIMENSIONAL ADHESIVE
Dimensional adhesive is a decorative adhesive that dries to a clear, shiny, raised surface, enhancing the colors applied underneath. (*See page 29*)

COLLAGE
A collage is a collection of artfully arranged stamped images, embellishments, and papers that is meaningful to the creator.
(*See page 84*)

DOUBLE-STAMPING
Double-stamping is the technique of stamping a single image on two different pieces of paper, then cutting out part of the second image and attaching it to the first.
(*See page 44*)

CRACKLE MEDIUM
Crackle medium is a two-part product that, when applied to a finished project, produces an antique, crackled look.
(*See page 115*)

DOUBLE-STICK ADHESIVE
Double-stick adhesive is a thin sheet with adhesive on both sides, each protected by a paper liner. When the liner is removed, the adhesive grabs glitter, leafing flakes, pieces of paper, or other decorative materials.
(*See page 107, right*)

CRIMPED PAPER
Crimped paper is paper that has straight or wavy ridges on one or both sides. Using a crimping tool produces double-sided ridges.
(*See page 65*)

DRY-PAINT PIGMENTS
Dry-paint pigments can be made into paint by adding them to gum arabic, or they can be added to other products to color backgrounds.
(*See page 75, left*)

EMBOSSING, DOUBLE

Double-embossing produces a glazed or stained-glass effect. The outline of a design is embossed, the inside colored, and the design embossed again with clear embossing powder. (*See page 96*)

INKING DIRECTLY ON PAPER

Ink can be applied directly to paper with a pad, sponge, stylus tips, and daubers. Pigment inks work best because they can be blended before they dry. (*See page 11, right*)

EMBOSSING, INK

Ink embossing is the process of raising an inked image by applying a special powder, which, when heated, rises up and becomes permanent. (*See page 99*)

LAYERING INK

Layering ink involves inking a stamp with a base color, then applying other colors over the first ink before stamping. This technique, also called double-inking, works best with metallic inks. (*See page 68, left*)

EMBOSSING, PAPER

Paper embossing is the technique of raising an image on paper using a metal stencil and stylus. (*See page 122, top*)

LAYERING PAPER

Layering paper is the process of framing an image by placing multiple papers behind. (*See page 59*)

EMBOSSING, RESIST

The technique of resist embossing lets you preserve the color of the background paper as part of the design. This is because any ink that is applied after embossing will wipe right off the embossed areas. (*See page 95, bottom*)

LIQUID APPLIQUÉ

Liquid appliqué adds dimension to a stamped image. Heat it immediately after application for a puffy "popcorn" effect. For an overall puffy look, let it stand for several hours then heat from below. For a suede effect, apply it with a brayer. (*See page 13*)

INKING STAMPS WITH MARKERS

Inking a stamp with a marker is a precise way to apply color to part of the stamp or the entire image. This is an especially useful technique when you want to blend colors on a stamp. (*See page 55, bottom*)

MASKING

Masking is the process of covering an image or the area around the image with fresh paper so that a second image can be stamped. Removing the mask reveals the second image in the background. (*See page 37, bottom*)

OVER-STAMPING
The process of over-stamping consists of stamping one image over another.
(*See page 36, left*)

RESIST PAPER
Resist paper is chemically treated paper that resists ink in certain places or patterns.
(*See page 124*)

PAINTING WITH RE-INKERS
Coloring images with the bottled ink designed to re-ink stamp pads results in exceptionally vivid colors.
(*See page 75, right*)

ROLLER STAMPS
Roller stamps are interchangeable, cylindrical stamps in a roller handle that can be inked with a separate inkpad or continuously with a built-in pad.
(*See page 85, bottom*)

POP-UP CONSTRUCTION
Pop-up construction is the technique of cutting, folding, and mounting an image so that when you open a card, the design pops up from the inside.
(*See page 16, both*)

STIPPLING
Stippling is the process of brushing on tiny dots of color with a stippling brush. Ink the stippling brush with dye ink from a brush marker or pad.
(*See page 83*)

PUNCH ART
Punch art is the process of using punched shapes as is or folding and combining them with other shapes to create new images. The negative space left behind by the punch is often as useful as the punched shape itself.
(*See page 110*)

TEA-BAG FOLDING
Tea-bag folding involves cutting papers to tea-bag size, then folding and assembling the papers into attractive designs.
(*See page 128*)

REPEAT STAMPING
Stamping the same image repeatedly can produce a pleasing, rhythmic design.
(*See page 78, top*)

WATERMARK
A watermark is a subtle tone-on-tone pattern on paper. You can duplicate this effect with watermark ink stamped on medium-toned paper.
(*See page 51, left*)

SOURCES

For products used call the companies for a retail store near you. If you do not have one available, most of the products and stamps may be purchased from The Great American Stamp Store, 203-221-1229.

If you are a retailer, most of the products, may be purchased wholesale from the Craft Connection, 203-338-9695.

SUPPLIERS

ANGELWING ENTERPRISES
915 W. Michigan
Fresno, CA 93705
559-241-7312

A STAMP IN THE HAND
20630 S. Leapwood Ave.
Suite B
Carson, CA 90746
310-329-8555

ALL NIGHT MEDIA
P.O. Box 10607
San Rafael, CA 94912
415-460-2064

AMY'S MAGIC
173 Main St.
West Leechburg, PA 15656
724-845-1748

ANN-TICIPATIONS
6852 Pacific Ave.
Suite D
Stockton, CA 95207
209-952-5538

ART IMPRESSIONS
6079 Trail Ave. NE
Keizer, OR 97303

BEEDZ/ART ACCENTS
960 Yew St.
Bellingham, WA 98226
877-733-8989

CLEARSNAP
Box 98
Anacortes, WA 98221
1-800-448-4862

CRAFTER'S PICK
The Adhesive Products, Inc.
520 Cleveland Ave.
Albany, CA 94710
1-800-766-7616

C-THRU RULER COMPANY
6 Britton Dr.
Bloomfield, CT 06002
860-243-0303

DENAMI DESIGNS
P.O. Box 5617
Kent, WA 98064
253-437-1626

DESIGN ORIGINALS
2425 Cullen St.
Fort Worth, TX 76107-1411

DR. PH. MARTIN'S
Salis International
4093 N. 28th Way
Hollywood, FL 33020
1-800-843-8293

DREAMWEAVER STENCILS
1335 Cindee Lane
Dept. A
Colton, CA 92324

EK SUCCESS
P.O. Box 1141
Clifton, NJ 07014
1-800-524-1349

EMAGINATION CRAFTS, INC.
630-238-9770
emaginationcraft.com

EMBOSSING ARTS CO., INC.
P.O. Box 439
Tangent, OR 97389

FAMILY TREASURES
24922 Anza Dr.
Unit A
Valencia, CA 91355
1-800-413-2645

FISKARS, INC.
1-800-950-0203
Fiskars.com

FRED B. MULLETT
P.O. Box 94502
Seattle, WA 98124
206-624-5723

GREAT AMERICAN STAMPS
1015 Post Road East
Westport, CT 06880
203-221-1229

HERO ARTS RUBBER STAMPS, INC.
1343 Powell St.
Emeryville, CA 94608
510-652-6055
heroarts.com

HER RUBBER
26395 S. Morgan Rd.
Estacada, OR 97023
503-630-3130

HOT POTATOES
2805 Columbine Place
Nashville, TN 37204
615-269-8002

IMPRESS
120 Andover Pk. E.
Tukwila, WA 98188

INKADINKADO
Woburn, MA 01801
718-938-6100

JUDIKINS
17803 S. Harvard Blvd.
Gardena, CA 90248
310-515-1115

KRYLON
31500 Solon Rd.
Solon, OH 44139
216-498-2300

LOVE TO STAMP
1125 Harrison Ave.
Centralia, WA 98531
360-736-9535

LUCKY SQUIRREL
P.O. Box 606
Belen, NM 87002
1-800-462-4912

LYRA
78 Browne St., Suite 3
Brookline, MA 02446
617-731-9851

MAGENTA
351 Blain
Mont-Saint-Hilaire
QC, Canada J3H 3BH

MARVY UCHIDA CORP.
1027 E. Burgrove St.
Carson, CA 90746

MCGILL, INC.
1-800-982-9884
Mcgillinc.com

NANKONG ENTERPRISES, INC.
Polly Drummond Center
Suite 16E
Newark, DE 19711
302-731-2995

OUTLINES RUBBER STAMPS
643 Middle Tpke.
Storrs, CT 06268
860-429-0362

PENNY BLACK, INC.
P.O. Box 11496
Berkeley, CA 94712
510-849-1883

PAPER PARACHUTE
P.O. Box 91385
Portland, OR 97291-0385

PERSONAL STAMP EXCHANGE (PSX)
360 Sutton Place
Santa Rosa, CA 95407
707-588-8058

PLAID ENTERPRISES, INC.
Norcross, GA 30091-7600

POSH IMPRESSIONS
22600-A Lambert St. #706
Lake Forest, CA 92630
1-800-421-7674

PRINTWORKS COLLECTION
12342 McCann Dr.
Santa Fe Springs, CA 90670

RENAISSANCE ART
P.O. Box 1218
Burlington, CT 06013

RIVER CITY RUBBER WORKS
555 S. Meridian
Wichita, KS 67217
316-529-8656

RUBBERMOON
P.O. Box 3258
Hayden Lake, ID 83835
208-772-9772

RUBBER STAMPS OF AMERICA
1-800-553-5031

SAVVY STAMPS
20146 Marine View Dr. S.W.
Seattle, WA 98166

SPEEDBALL ART PRODUCTS CO.
P.O. Box 5157
Statesville, NC 28687
704-838-1475

STAMP CABANA
352 Park Avenue S.
Winter Park, FL 32789
407-628-8863

STAMPA ROSA, INC.
60 Maxwell Ct.
Santa Rosa, CA 95401
1-800-554-5744

STAMPASSIONS, INC.
10316 Norris Ave.
Suite A
Pacoima, CA 91331
1-800-ART-STAMP

STAMPENDOUS
1-800-869-0474
stampendous.com

STAMPINGTON & COMPANY
22992 Mill Creek
Suite B
Laguna Hills, CA 92653

STAMP IT!
317 Laskin Rd.
Virginia Beach, VA 23451
757-425-0721

THERM O WEB
1-800-323-0799

TSUKINEKO, INC.
15411 N.E. 95th St.
Redmond, WA 98052
425-883-7733

PROJECT MATERIALS

PAGE 6
(*Left*)
Stamps—Impress
Inks—Marvy Uchida, Tsukineko
(*Right*)
Stamps—Personal Stamp
   Exchange, Stampa Rosa
Inks—Tsukineko, Clearsnap,
   Dr. Ph. Martin's
Misc.—Krylon Paint Pen

PAGE 7
(*Left*)
Stamps—Personal Stamp Exchange
Inks—Clearsnap
(*Right*)
Stamps—Magenta
Inks—Clearsnap

PAGE 9
(*Left*)
Stamps—Printworks Collection
Inks—Marvy Uchida
(*Right*)
Stamps—Magenta
Inks—Clearsnap
Misc.—Clearsnap Stylus Tool

PAGE 10
(*Left*)
Stamps—Clearsnap Rollagraph
Inks—Clearsnap, Dr. Ph. Martin's
Punches—Emagination Crafts
Misc.—Design Originals Instructions
(*Right*)
Stamps—Impress
Inks—Tsukineko

PAGE 11
(*Left*)
Stamps—Inkadinkado
Inks—Clearsnap, Marvy Uchida
(*Right*)
Inks—Clearsnap
Punches—McGill

PAGE 12
(*Left*)
Stamps—Hot Potatoes
Inks—Clearsnap, Dr. Ph. Martin's
Papers—Hot Potatoes
Misc.—Posh Impressions Sponge
(*Right*)
Stamps—A Stamp In The Hand
Punches—McGill
Misc.—Amy's Magic Leafing Flakes
   and Adhesive

PAGE 13
Stamps—Embossing Arts, All Night
   Media
Inks—Clearsnap, Marvy Uchida
Punches—Emagination Crafts
Misc.—JudiKins Embossing
   Powder, Amy's Magic Glitter,
   Marvy Uchida Liquid Appliqué

PAGE 14
(*Left*)
Stamps—Fred B. Mullett
Inks—Clearsnap
Misc.—JudiKins Embossing Powder
(*Right*)
Stamps—Hero Arts
Inks—Clearsnap
Punches—McGill
Misc.—JudiKins Embossing Powder

PAGE 15
(*Left*)
Stamps—Magenta
Inks—Clearsnap
Misc.—Clearsnap Stylus Tools
(*Right*)
Stamps—Impress
Inks—Clearsnap

PAGE 16
(*Left*)
Stamps—Penny Black
Inks—Clearsnap
(*Right*)
Stamps—Embossing Arts Co.
Inks—Clearsnap
Misc.—EK Success Circle Scissors

PAGE 17
(*Top*)
Stamps—Printworks Collection
Inks—Marvy Uchida
Punches—McGill, Marvy Uchida
Misc.—Amy's Magic Glitter, Fiskars
   Paper Edgers
(*Bottom*)
Stamps—JudiKins
Inks—Clearsnap
Misc.—JudiKins Embossing Powder

PAGE 18
Punches—Marvy Uchida
Misc.—Fiskars Paper Edgers

PAGE 19
Stamps—Printworks Collection,
   All Night Media, Stampassions
Inks—Marvy Uchida
Punches—Marvy Uchida
Misc.—Amy's Magic Glitter,
   Fiskars Paper Edgers, Marvy
   Uchida White Gel Pen

PAGE 20
(*Left*)
Stamps—Personal Stamp Exchange
Inks—Tsukineko, Marvy Uchida
Misc.— Lucky Squirrel Clear
   PolyShrink™
(*Right*)
Inks—Tsukineko, Marvy Uchida

PAGE 21
Stamps—Magenta
Inks—Clearsnap

PAGE 22
Stamps—Magenta
Inks—Tsukineko

PAGE 23
Stamps—Hero Arts
Inks—Tsukineko, Clearsnap
Papers—JudiKins MatteKote
   Cardstock
Punches—Fiskars Corner Punch
Misc.—Fiskars Crimper and Brayer

PAGE 24
Stamps—Impress
Inks—Tsukineko, Clearsnap,
   Marvy Uchida
Misc.—Impress Eyelets